Prove It!

Prove It!

Achieving Quality Recognition for Your Early Childhood Program

Rachel Robertson and Miriam Dressler

Redleaf Press®
www.redleafpress.org
800-423-8309

Published by Redleaf Press
10 Yorkton Court
St. Paul, MN 55117
www.redleafpress.org

First edition 2010
Cover design by Erin New
Interior typeset in Whitman and designed by Mayfly Design
Printed in the United States of America
16 15 14 13 12 11 10 09   1 2 3 4 5 6 7 8

Library of Congress Cataloging-in-Publication Data
Robertson, Rachel.
  Prove it! : achieving quality recognition for your early childhood program / Rachel Robertson and Miriam Dressler.
     p. cm.
  Includes bibliographical references.
  ISBN 978-1-933653-77-8
1. Education, Preschool—United States—Evaluation. 2. Education, Preschool—Standards—United States. 3. Accreditation (Education)—United States. 4. Day care centers—United States—Evaluation. I. Dressler, Miriam. II. Title.
  LB1140.23.R64 2010
  372.21—dc22

                              2009021337

Printed on FSC certified paper

FSC
Mixed Sources
Product group from well-managed forests and other controlled sources
Cert no. SW-COC-002283
www.fsc.org
© 1996 Forest Stewardship Council

All children deserve the absolute best adults can give them. We offer this book to all those who won't settle for less and dedicate themselves to this mission every day.

RACHEL

To the teachers that have given their best
to my children. And to my daughters.

MIRIAM

To my near and dear ones, and to all the incredible center directors
who believe that small things make a big difference.

Prove It!

Prove It! Activities

Preface

Accreditation, quality rating systems, environmental rating scales—these phrases are heard, discussed, and increasingly valued in the world of early care and education. Resources to measure outcomes have expanded in recent years and our knowledge has grown regarding the impact early care experiences can have on children. With that information, providers of early care and education are, and should be, held more accountable for meeting standards that have been found to ensure important rich, meaningful experiences for young children. But that doesn't mean meeting standards is easy. Being committed to the outcome doesn't mean you have to be enthused about the process. If you have this book in your hands, it is likely you are leading an early childhood program and have chosen, or have been asked, to embark on a journey to achieve a third-party quality endorsement for your center or program. Many people in your position have mixed feelings about beginning such a task. This is undeniably a huge undertaking, one that will surely take hours and hours of your time. It will also, most likely, significantly change the way you understand and provide care for young children. Fortunately, a desire to meet this objective is all you need to begin— to ensure your impact on children is the best it can be.

After all, that's what we first brought to the task. We've come to writing this book after both having had the privilege, and sometimes admittedly, the angst, of leading programs through a third-party quality endorsement system. Rachel's first "grown-up" job was as a YMCA camp director, and she went through accreditation that very first summer, barely understanding what the word *accreditation* even meant. Her first experience in an accredited early childhood program was in a center accredited by the National Association for the Education of Young Children (NAEYC) where everyone seemed to speak in a foreign language, comparing all they planned and did with the children to the NAEYC standards. Rachel quickly learned the value of having standards to adhere to as the center maintained its accreditation and then pursued reaccreditation.

Miriam's first experience with third-party quality endorsement was overwhelming and confusing. Upon accepting a center director position and starting to learn the ropes, she was handed a box of materials by a colleague and told, "Hey, good news, your visit is in August." It was already March! Reading the materials, Miriam very quickly realized that little or no self-study had been done prior to submitting the request for a visit. What followed were a lot of late nights, sudden changes, staff turnover, and stress. The lesson she learned was that third-party quality endorsement should not be rushed or faked, and although the center achieved accreditation, those standards were very difficult to maintain because the only people who had any real buy-in were Miriam and the assistant director. She has since spent her time helping others equip themselves with the knowledge and tools necessary to avoid those mistakes.

More recently, we (the authors) worked together with a team of professionals dedicated to supporting more than 1,700 centers through the process of accreditation. Currently we work as consultants for programs and organizations that offer guidance and support to other programs. We're also validators for some of the national accreditations and have served on task forces or focus groups dedicated to developing or enhancing criteria. In other words, we both have been there, done that, and know that the late nights, hair pulling, and paperwork chaos are worth it in the end. And we know that the children in your care will be better off because of the effort and commitment you make.

Regardless of your feelings as you embark on this journey, it still remains an often confusing and time-consuming process. Time and again center directors and program administrators share their frustration with us over the details involved in the process and their lack of time to address each detail adequately. This has nothing to do with their commitment and dedication to the process. As one director put it, "Is there any other choice but to be accredited? If it is what is best for children how could I ever consider *not* doing it?" She said this as she sat on the floor in her office at nine o'clock at night matching evidence to criteria amid stacks and stacks of paper.

The challenge is not so much in convincing the early childhood education community of the value that lies in pursuing and achieving third-party quality endorsement, but rather how to prepare and provide resources and offer support for those going through the process so they can feel successful in their work—developing systems, accessing tools, and leading a team effectively and knowledgeably through this complex process. Equally important, many individuals leading a program through a third-party quality endorsement system lose their work-life balance. We hope using this book helps you to never, ever have to make a choice between pursuing a third-party quality endorsement and having a family life, hobbies, or even keeping your plants alive.

This book is for you. We want the thoughts, advice, and ideas in this book to be meaningful to you and adaptable to your needs while maintaining the integrity of the systems we discuss. Each chapter will focus on an important aspect of the process and will provide definitions, context, and practical tools and resources. Details appear in the chapter summaries, beginning on page 1. Collectively we have spent a number of years determining the best approaches and tools needed to succeed when pursuing an early childhood third-party quality endorsement system, such as accreditation or an environment rating scale. We have worked through this important process with hundreds of early childhood programs and have garnered valuable wisdom and ideas from each of them. We have been fortunate to see the amazing transformations that can occur on behalf of children, families, and staff as programs progress. We also know that achieving and maintaining standards set forth by a quality endorsement system can make a significant difference in a child's life, which is the early childhood educator's ultimate goal.

Granted, it is ideal to have a mentor or friend by your side as you delve into a process such as this, as it is with any challenging, time-consuming, and often confusing process. We intend this book to be the next best thing to that mentor or friend for those tasked with leading a program through a quality measurement and endorsement system. This book is not meant to replace the official materials and tools that are part of the third-party quality endorsement system you are pursuing. Consider it a supplement that shares tips, ideas, definitions, and other practical advice. We intend for this book to be *used*. Our hope is that you read it, write in the margins, highlight, copy pages, flag helpful hints, doodle—whatever helps you process, understand, make connections, and ultimately succeed. Throughout this book you'll find tools, evaluations, activities, and more, all aimed at helping you understand, prepare, progress, and achieve, so that you will reach the day when you can dance around and say, "We achieved our goal! We did it!"

At this point, that day may seem a long way off, but we intend to help you get there. Whether this is your first encounter with the process (and someone else told you that you had to do it) or you have chosen to embark on this journey for the fourth or fifth time in your career, the tools and resources in this book will assist you. Third-party quality endorsement systems continue to evolve and change as new research becomes available and as new technology or resources are applied, making it virtually impossible for someone to rely only on their prior experience to support them through the process. Actually, in recent years, prior experience has become quite an impediment. We have seen dozens of center directors struggle unnecessarily because they did not adequately acquaint themselves with a new system, relying instead on their hard-earned but outdated prior knowledge. Additionally, one of the most notable residual effects of going through a self-evaluation process is personal growth and development. Each time you go through the process, you learn something new or different. Each time the experience can be rich and meaningful for you and can stimulate new ideas and processes resulting in positive impacts in the program for children. Not requesting support when going through this process a subsequent time is akin to saying you don't need a friend to go out to dinner with you because the last time you went out to dinner you had a friend and now you don't need one anymore. Our hope is that this time, along with being rich and meaningful, will also be easier as you use this book to support your journey.

Although the book's intended audience is program directors and administrators, teachers and program staff will surely be affected by the process as well. A broad range of skill level, knowledge, and experience in the field exists regardless of position. Along with varied levels of familiarity with third-party quality endorsement systems, these differences mean everyone involved will have a unique experience and contribute in different ways while they share and pursue this common goal.

Pursuing a third-party quality endorsement system is a significant undertaking. Whether it is something the center has experienced many times before or it is the first attempt, the tasks and objectives are noteworthy. There is no perfect way to achieve the goals of the third-party quality endorsement system; what is important is to simply achieve them. The steps and support found in this book were developed based on real needs and requests from center directors and other key stakeholders. Whether you go through each chapter sequentially or skip around, the level of care and consideration you will be able to apply to each step will ensure that the impact of the third-party quality endorsement system is more than a certificate on the wall. Instead, it will be truly pervasive and long-lasting, ensuring high quality in all you do for children.

Acknowledgments

Words don't just fall effortlessly on a page and suddenly become a book. Much effort is put into the process and without the help and support of many, our words would not have made it here.

We would like to thank Kyra Ostendorf for knowing we were the right authors for the task and making this opportunity possible, David Heath and Jean Cook for their comprehensive and detailed editing efforts, and the QI team who we miss greatly. We know many of our ideas and much of our knowledge stem from the work we did together.

Introduction

Using This Book

We don't expect you will want to read this book from cover to cover. Instead you'll probably pick and choose information that fits your situation. First we provide summaries of each chapter so that you can easily find those that apply to you. Next we introduce you to the Sunshine Child Development Center, a fictional center we created to provide examples of the tasks you may face working on a third-party quality endorsement. Then we provide a list of the major third-party quality endorsement systems. This section ends with a list of common terms and their definitions. We felt that these would be more useful up front rather than in a glossary at the end of the book.

Chapter Summaries

Part 1: Preparing for the Process

This section introduces ideas, concepts, and knowledge that are vital as you consider and then commit to a third-party quality endorsement system.

CHAPTER 1: DEFINING THIRD-PARTY QUALITY ENDORSEMENT SYSTEMS

This chapter provides an overview of third-party quality endorsement systems—what they are and why they are valuable to the early care and education field. Chapter 1 details different options and includes a readiness assessment to help you reach a better understanding of your program's level of preparedness as you begin the process.

CHAPTER 2: CHOOSING A THIRD-PARTY QUALITY ENDORSEMENT SYSTEM

This chapter guides you in thinking through all of the variables you must consider when deciding to pursue a third-party quality endorsement system. Whether you've already chosen a third-party quality endorsement system to pursue or are still considering the options, it is imperative to consider the reasons for pursuing a quality endorsement before you begin ensuring a higher level of commitment to the goal.

CHAPTER 3: YOUR ROLE AS THE LEADER

A common and often detrimental mistake many programs make is not giving careful consideration to the needs of the teaching team. Much of the focus is on the children—as it should be—and the adults may get lost in the process. The unfortunate result is often a lack of commitment or buy-in. Considering the needs of the adults and how best to create a culture of change before beginning the process is one of the single best advantages you can give your program. Chapter 3 focuses on how you can communicate with, support, and lead your teaching team.

CHAPTER 4: PROFESSIONAL DEVELOPMENT

The knowledge, abilities, and skills of the caregivers in your program often have a direct link to the quality of care provided for the children. Accreditation and quality rating systems criteria increasingly emphasize professional development, which supports higher levels of skill and knowledge for early childhood professionals. Chapter 4 examines those criteria and discusses ways to support your staff in their pursuit of professional development, whether it be enthusiastically or reluctantly.

Part 2: The Process

This section focuses on the process of pursuing and achieving a third-party quality endorsement. Each chapter is dedicated to a different aspect of the process leading to a complete understanding of what, why, and how to succeed.

CHAPTER 5: OVERVIEW OF THE SELF-STUDY PROCESS

The time spent evaluating your program, collecting evidence, making improvements, and completing paperwork is considered to be the self-study period. Research tells us that this course of action has an impact in and of itself and should be valued as such. This time should not be considered just a means to an end. That said, a complete understanding of the process and its intent will ensure that steps aren't skipped and or rushed.

CHAPTER 6: USING THE SELF-STUDY MATERIALS

Many good center directors find themselves stuck after reviewing the self-study requirements. They have everyone on board, they know what they're doing, and they have all the materials. Then they wonder, "Now what?" This chapter presents some practical first steps to get going in the right direction. Now that you're armed with a deeper understanding of the processes and approaches toward achieving all that needs to be done, we show you how to put those things into action. Developing a practical and achievable timeline and action plans is a learned skill—chapter 6 provides insight and tips into doing that well.

Part 3: The Content

This section examines the most common and important content areas shared among third-party quality endorsement systems. The chapters in this section have similar formats but focus on their respective content areas by defining what each topic means and demonstrating how to implement the content areas in a real setting. They make connections between criteria and real-life situations and provide suggestions for implementation and tools for evaluation.

CHAPTER 7: PHYSICAL ENVIRONMENT

The physical environment can be thought of as an additional teacher if set up and used correctly. A well-designed classroom can increase learning and enrich a child's experience. Chapter 7 focuses on indoor and outdoor facilities and equipment, detailing how to set up, utilize, and evaluate the learning environments children experience each day.

CHAPTER 8: HEALTH AND SAFETY

Health and safety are a primary focus for most third-party quality endorsement systems. Above all, children must be protected. Without a healthy and safe environment it is futile to focus on anything else. Chapter 8 concentrates on both policy and implementation and will help center directors understand common standards and why they are important.

CHAPTER 9: TEACHING AND LEARNING

This chapter addresses the important relationships in the program and the methods used to teach young children. The focus is on the full circle of opportunities for learning and development in an early care and education setting and how teachers plan for, implement, and individualize those opportunities using curriculum, assessment, and spontaneous teachable moments.

Chapter 10: Assessment of Learning and Development

Observation and assessment have become increasingly valued in early childhood. While assessment is multifaceted, it doesn't have to be complicated. Chapter 10 describes the value of assessing children's learning as the final step in closing the learning and teaching cycle. It includes practical information on how to incorporate simple, yet effective, observation and assessment practices into your program to meet the requirements of your third-party quality endorsement system.

Chapter 11: Family and Community Involvement

A program pursuing a third-party quality endorsement system cannot succeed or truly achieve the highest quality of care without including the families and connecting to the greater community. Chapter 11 focuses on specific ways program staff can optimize those relationships.

Part 4: What's Next?

This section examines actions the program staff need to complete prior to, during, and following the on-site assessment visit. In the self-study process, a critical error often occurs after receiving the decision from the third-party quality endorsement system: adopting the attitude that the work is done when the visit is over. That is false—the work has just begun. Maintaining high standards of care takes daily commitment and effort. The chapters in this section discuss the immediate work of responding to results and feedback provided by the third-party quality endorsement system and the long-term work of maintaining high quality every day.

Chapter 12: The On-Site Assessment Visit

The self-study is over and an on-site visit has been requested. Then the waiting begins. Chapter 12 focuses on the work that should happen during this time, including some important tips for handling the actual visit and what should happen when you get the results. Whether the outcome is positive or negative, it is important to know how to react and what to do with the information you receive.

Chapter 13: Maintaining Quality Standards

You did it—you achieved your goal! All that hard work paid off. Now all you have to do is keep it up for, well, forever. Chapter 13 shares tips and strategies for keeping staff members focused on the high quality standards they worked so hard to meet, including information on how best to introduce new staff to your program's standards and expectations.

Model Program: Sunshine Child Development Center

We use examples throughout the text in an effort to bring the process to life. With our collective experience and the information we have gathered from working with hundreds of centers, we created a fictional program representing a combination of typical characteristics—the Sunshine Child Development Center.

Sunshine Child Development Center
Five classrooms: Infant, Toddler, Twos, Preschool, Prekindergarten
Center staff:

- Martha, center director
- Georgia, assistant center director
- Julio, preK teacher
- Magda, preK teacher
- Isabel, preschool teacher
- Chae, preschool teacher
- Jessica, infant teacher
- Elena, infant teacher
- Patrice, assistant infant teacher
- Shondra, toddler teacher
- Natalie, toddler teacher
- Renate, assistant toddler teacher
- Mizuki, floater

Martha is a relatively new center director (CD), having started at the center six months ago. She has her associate degree in early childhood education. The center is full and the staff has taken that as a sign that change is not necessary. Nevertheless, the board wants Martha to achieve an accreditation of her choice within two years.

Martha and the team at the Sunshine Child Development Center will go on this accreditation journey with you. In each chapter, we will begin by describing their challenges and progress and then help you think about yours.

Third-Party Quality Endorsement Systems

Because so many third-party quality endorsement systems are available to early childhood providers, we try to use general language whenever possible. But the advice and direction suggested throughout the book is relevant to many systems, particularly those listed here. If the advice doesn't apply generally, we say so. When it seems useful, we provide examples to illustrate a point, not to endorse any particular system or tool. Please review the names and acronyms below to become familiar with the systems we considered and studied while writing this book and the few we chose to use for examples. We focused on systems that currently operate nationally, primarily work with early childhood organizations, and are, at minimum, part of at least two state systems.

AMS: American Montessori Society: www.amshq.org/schools_accreditation.htm#

APPLE: Accredited Professional Preschool Learning Environment: www.faccm.org/apple.asp

Arnett Caregiver Interaction Scale: www.acf.hhs.gov/programs/opre/ehs/perf_measures/reports/resources_measuring/res_meas_impa.html

ASCI: Association of Christian Schools International: www.acsi.org

CITA: Commission on International Trans-Regional Accreditation: www.citaschools.org

CLASS: Classroom Assessment Scoring System: www.classobservation.com

COA: Council on Accreditation: www.coanet.org

ECERS: Early Childhood Environment Rating Scale (preschool): www.fpg.unc.edu/~ECERS/

ERS: Environment Rating Scale: www.fpg.unc.edu/~ECERS/

ITERS: Infant/Toddler Environment Rating Scale: www.fpg.unc.edu/~ECERS/

NAA: National AfterSchool Association: www.naaweb.org

NAC: National Accreditation Commission: www.naccp.org

NACCP: National Association of Child Care Professionals (sponsoring organization of NAC): www.naccp.org

NAECP: National Accreditation for Early Childhood Professionals (a term that refers to NAEYC's accreditation system but is rarely used): www.naeyc.org

NAEYC: National Association for the Education of Young Children: www.naeyc.org/

NAFCC: National Association for Family Child Care: www.nafcc/ accreditation/accreditation.asp

NECPA: National Early Childhood Program Accreditation: www.necpa.net

PAS: Program Administration Scale: http://cecl.nl.edu/evaluation/pas.htm

QRS or QRIS: Quality Rating System/Quality Rating and Improvement System: http://nccic.acf.hhs.gov

SACERS: School-Age Care Environment Rating Scale: www.fpg.unc .edu/~ecers/

Definitions

Here are some common terms and definitions we use throughout the text.

caregiver Anyone providing care for and teaching children; used synonymously with **teacher**.

center director (CD) Anyone charged with primary management and leadership tasks; used synonymously with **program administrator** or **administrator**.

criteria A defined measure or expectation. Some third-party quality endorsement systems use the term synonymously with **standard** and some do not (we do throughout this text). It is important to know this about your chosen third-party quality endorsement system to avoid confusion. Also, can be used synonymously with **indicator**.

early care and education One of many phrases used to describe our field. When we refer to early care and education programs we include child care, learning centers, child development centers and more; used synonymously with **early childhood education** or **child care**.

family Any members of the child's family; used synonymously with **family members**.

key stakeholders Any individuals or groups who are invested in the success of your center, including governing board members, parent forum members, senior or executive leadership, and/or staff and families.

parent Always paired with guardian to encompass all individuals legally charged with the care of a child.

program Any entity providing care and education for children in early childhood; used synonymously with **center**.

self-study The period of time beginning when a program "enrolls" or orders materials and ending with their on-site visit.

submission When a program sends in documentation or another necessary procedure required by the third-party quality endorsement system to indicate they are ready for a visit.

third-party quality endorsement system A phrase used to encompass any external system an early childhood program uses to assess their program quality; used synonymously with **quality measurement and endorsement system**, or **third-party endorsement system**.

validator The representative of the third-party quality endorsement system who visits your program and observes and records findings to be measured against criteria or standards. Each third-party quality endorsement system has its own term—we use *validator* in this book. Can be synonymous with **assessor**, **verifier**, **representative**, **reviewer**, or **endorser**.

Part 1
Preparing for the Process

It is tempting to jump right in and start doing the work when tasked with a large project. Yet this is most often a harmful approach. In our experience, programs that plan carefully and act purposefully have a much higher success rate. And not only is the success rate higher, but sustaining the high quality achieved during the third-party quality endorsement system process is more assured.

This section will help you understand the purpose of a third-party quality endorsement system, recognize the differences among systems, determine how to choose the program that best suits your needs, recognize your role as a leader, and consider approaches toward professional development for staff.

All of these topics should be thoroughly and completely understood before embarking on this busy, exciting, challenging, and rewarding journey.

Defining Third-Party Quality Endorsement Systems

Being new both to her role at the Sunshine Center and to the role of center director, Martha doesn't know a lot about leading a center through the accreditation process. She is sure she has enough to do without adding this work to her plate. But the center's board insists, and she wants to be successful. Martha knows that accreditation is supposed to help the center achieve high quality, but she and many of the staff members believe it already offers high-quality care. She taught at a center that had gone through accreditation by the National Association for the Education of Young Children (NAEYC), but that was years ago, and she's heard the system has changed. Additionally, she finds that her state recognizes more national accreditation choices as part of its Quality Rating System (QRS) than before. She remembers that accreditation took a significant amount of time. She wants to get started, but doesn't know how. She decides she needs to learn more about accreditation and her choices.

What Is a Third-Party Quality Endorsement System?

Most fields of education have systems that measure and endorse quality. From colleges to supplemental/tutoring organizations, educators, students, and families rely on the ratings to indicate and measure levels of quality. In the early childhood field we have a variety of quality measurement and endorsement systems including accreditation systems, rating scales, and individual component assessments. The intent of these systems is often twofold: to provide a tool that defines the standards of high quality early care and education and a service that helps programs serving young children pursue and achieve those same standards.

Each state has its own licensing regulations—agreed-upon minimum levels of care that programs must provide in order to operate. Among the states, licensing regulations may vary in terms of how stringent they are. Typically, these regulations focus primarily on health and safety. Licensing compliance is a requirement of all quality endorsement systems.

In addition to licensing, many programs are committed to meeting internally developed organizational standards and criteria, regardless of whether the program is a privately owned center, a government facility, a nonprofit, or a for-profit organization. Often these criteria are broader than licensing regulations and may include operating and fiscal policies, staff education and professional development requirements, and education content and delivery standards, among other things.

Accreditation, ERS, QRS, and other quality endorsement systems represent the next level. Programs pursuing approval at this level must successfully meet licensing and typical organizational requirements in order to satisfy the quality standards and enhanced practices.

Levels of Quality Endorsement

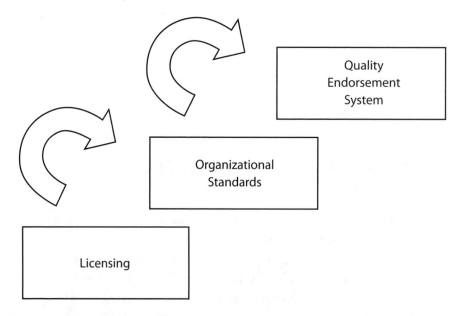

While each of the third-party quality endorsement systems has a unique approach and distinct characteristics, they also have much in common. After all, the qualities that research indicates are best for children's development and education are often universally accepted. In the field of early care and education, the quality endorsement systems that measure and endorse quality focus on some consistent aspects:

- health and safety
- curriculum design and delivery
- educational and developmental opportunities in all domains (emotional, social, cognitive, physical, and approaches to learning)
- teaching methods and strategies
- relationships between teachers and children, teachers and family members, teachers and management, management and families, and so on
- child assessment
- professional development for staff
- sound management policies and practices
- family involvement
- community resources and connections
- physical environment

Each of these components has an impact on the quality of care for young children. As with any puzzle, if a piece is missing, no matter how small, the final outcome will not be complete.

Each system has its own approach to program evaluation. Some share more characteristics than others. Professionals trained and endorsed by or on behalf of each system evaluate a program's practices in relation to standards or criteria by using some or all of the following methods: reviewing work samples, collecting data, observing classrooms, and surveying or interviewing families and staff.

These topics are addressed by specific criteria or standards that require evidence proving the program adequately meets them. Research has shown the importance of determining both the structural components of a program (such as staff/child ratios, building design, education or professional development of staff) and the procedural components (such as teaching methods, interactions in the classroom, and curriculum delivery).

Additionally, each system has its own structure, both in terms of how programs proceed through a self-study process and how programs are evaluated. The steps or phases embedded in each system need to be completed fully and sequentially to ensure success. The following sections provide brief overviews of the most commonly used early childhood third-party quality endorsement systems.

National Association for the Education of Young Children (NAEYC)

www.naeyc.org

History

NAEYC began in the 1920s as the National Association for Nursery Education, a group focused on the quality in available programs. They developed their accreditation system in the 1980s and have revised it periodically to reflect current research and practices. NAEYC also holds national conferences, publishes books and magazines, and is a leading voice in early childhood public policy and advocacy both nationally and internationally.

Scope

NAEYC accredits programs serving children from six weeks old to kindergarten age.

Distinctive Features

The accreditation system was revised and newly implemented in 2006. The process has four steps:

1. Enrollment: entry into self-study
2. Application: commitment to the accreditation process
3. Candidacy: completion of most of the preparation and submission of paperwork showing evidence of readiness for visit
4. Accreditation decision: on-site visit and assessment of criteria compliance

The system includes qualification requirements for administrators and staff at the candidacy level, as well as additional classifications of measurable criteria. There are four types of criteria:

1. Required: always assessed, must be met to achieve accreditation
2. Always: assessed on every visit to every program
3. Random: assessed randomly at different programs
4. Emergent: criteria that earn a program "extra credit" because they reflect new and evolving best practices

Other features:

- Programs seeking new accreditation can develop their own timeline for completion.
- Accredited centers are subject to unannounced visits during the term of accreditation.
- The accreditation term is five years regardless of whether the program is pursuing new accreditation or reaccreditation.

National Association of Child Care Professionals (NACCP)/ National Accreditation Commission (NAC)

www.naccp.org

History

NACCP was established in 1984 with the goal of supporting child care center directors in leading and managing quality programs. NAC accreditation is a part of the NACCP. NAC plans to release a revision of their materials in 2009; however, programs will be using the 2007 version for up to two more years depending on the date materials are ordered.

Scope

NAC accredits programs serving children from six weeks old through school age. They also have an optional faith-based component that lists standards specifically for Christian programs, as well as self-study materials available in Spanish.

Distinctive Features

The process has three steps:

1. Self-study: the period of time between ordering the materials and completing the evaluation and improvement process.
2. Validation: when a NAC validator visits the program and records their findings and observations.
3. Review and decision: accreditation is granted, denied, or deferred (which requires follow-up before the decision is finalized). NAC will make the accreditation decision and inform the program.

Other features:

- Centers seeking new accreditation must wait at least six months after ordering materials, but no longer than two years, to submit documentation.
- Accredited centers are subject to unannounced visits during the term of accreditation.
- The accreditation term is three years regardless of whether the program is pursuing new accreditation or reaccreditation.

National Early Childhood Program Accreditation (NECPA)

www.necpa.net

History

NECPA was started in 1992 as an independent accreditation system. NECPA plans to release a revision of their materials in 2009. However, because materials do not expire, many programs will be pursuing accreditation using previous versions for a few more years.

Scope

NECPA evaluates programs serving children from six weeks old to school age.

Distinctive Features

The process has three steps:

1. Self-study: the period of time between ordering the materials and completing the evaluation and improvement process.
2. On-site visit: when a verifier from NECPA visits the program and records their findings and observations.
3. Review and decision: accreditation is granted, denied, or pending (which requires follow-up before the decision is finalized). NECPA will make the accreditation decision within a specified time frame and inform the program.

Other features:

- Programs seeking new accreditation can develop their own timeline for completion.
- The accreditation term is three years regardless of whether a center is pursuing new accreditation or reaccreditation.

Environmental Rating Scales (ERS) (includes ITERS, ECERS, SACERS)

www.fpg.unc.edu/~ECERS/

History

Thelma Harms, Richard Clifford, and Debbie Cryer developed the original ERS in 1980. A revised edition was published in 1998.

Scope

ERS is the all-encompassing title for the infant/toddler scale (ITERS), the preschool scale (ECERS), and the school-age scale (SACERS). There is also an ERS for family child care. Revised versions created in 1998 are titled ITERS-R and ECERS-R, which are the only editions used in this book and used currently in third-party quality endorsement systems.

Distinctive Features

- The scales are scored differently from the accreditation systems. Programs receive a score on each item instead of a verified/nonverified rating. A specific rubric is attached to the scoring to contribute to more reliable ratings.
- Training on administering and interpreting the scales is offered annually for anyone interested.
- The scales are used in many ways—as stand-alone tools, as components of a state QRS, in the military child care system, in Head Start programs, and in much research.
- A center's score doesn't have an expiration date, that is, there is no set length of time for renewal. Each entity using the ERS scores (such as a state QRS) makes that determination.

- A university in Britain developed the ECERS-E. This version has more curriculum-focused criteria, and while not yet widely used, it addresses an area the ERS systems have been sometimes critiqued as lacking.
- The system (QRS, military, Head Start, and so on) using the ERS determines acceptable ratings, the self-study process, and technical support.

Other Systems

Additional systems exist and many states and organizations use them. At this time, however, most are not as widely used or applicable to many programs, so we do not cover them in detail. If you are using another system, such as one of those listed below, you will find that much of the guidance and information in this book pertains to these systems as well.

National AfterSchool Association (NAA)

www.naaweb.org

Council on Accreditation (CoA)

www.coanet.org
The NAA has partnered with the COA to provide an accreditation for after-school or school-age programs. COA also offers additional options for early childhood programs.

National Association for Family Child Care (NAFCC)

www.nafcc.org
NAFCC provides accreditation for family or at-home child care.

Commission on International Trans-Regional Accreditation (CITA)

www.citaschools.org
CITA provides accreditation for a multitude of educational contexts, such as enrichment classes, tutoring providers, and colleges and universities, and has recently begun to include early childhood education.

State-Specific Accreditations

Some states have also developed their own accreditation programs, such as the Accredited Professional Preschool Learning Environment (APPLE) in Florida and the Missouri Accreditation in Missouri.

Additionally, quality measurement tools are available for use to complement the full systems or to serve as steps toward a higher rating. The Program Administration Scale (PAS), Classroom Assessment Scoring System (CLASS), and the Arnett Caregiver Interaction Scale can all be useful measures of specialized components of program quality.

State QRS or QRIS

More than seventeen states currently have established a Quality Rating System (QRS) or Quality Rating Improvement System (QRIS) and many others are working toward developing such systems (see http://nccic.acf.hhs.gov for the current listing). The systems differ from state to state, but all are working toward the same goal—increasing the quality of care provided for children. States are becoming more involved in setting standards as research continually points to the long-term benefits of high-quality early childhood education for children and for the positive financial impact on the community as a whole over time. Regardless of the name (scale, accreditation, or rating system), the function is the same—to rate and assess the current quality of the program.

Why Pursue a Third-Party Quality Endorsement?

When considering accreditation or another measure of quality, many programs pose questions such as "What's in it for me?" or "Why go through all that effort when we already know we are high quality?" Conversely, others say, "Accreditation assures me that we are following the best and most current research for child development" or "Having someone else come in and validate that what we're doing is right for children; that's the key to ensuring our commitment and integrity."

Regardless of a child care program's initial assumptions or attitudes toward quality endorsement systems, it is important to understand the facts, details, and benefits of any quality endorsement system before starting such a journey. A successful program will ensure it understands each step and all details to fully commit and reap the highest benefits from the experience.

Quality measurement and endorsement systems have done much research to verify and validate that their materials and systems do in fact help programs increase and maintain the level of quality they are committed to for children. Through these efforts, the systems have made necessary alterations and improvements to ensure that they meet their intended objectives and continue to meet the needs of children and programs.

- The National AfterSchool Association encourages accreditation and argues that it leads to a better trained workforce, greater stability, and ultimately better outcomes for children and youth. Programs reap the benefits from well-trained staff members who typically transfer this knowledge when they move to other programs.
- NAEYC provides information for parents looking for high-quality child care: "NAEYC has developed 10 standards for high-quality early childhood education. Programs that meet these standards provide a safe and healthy environment for children, have teachers who are well-trained, have access to excellent teaching materials, and work with curriculum that is appropriately challenging and developmentally sound." (NAEYC n.d., 2)
- NECPA provides details about how its accreditation makes an impact: "The NECPA has been carefully crafted to create broad public understanding of the benefits of high quality early childhood care and education. Coupled with this increased understanding is a raised awareness of the 'professional expertise' required to deliver that high quality care and an appreciation of the advantages that children receive from accredited centers and schools." (National Early Childhood Program Accreditation 2005)

Of course, each system is biased when promoting its resources and process. So it is important to look to outside studies or evaluations of quality measurement and evaluation systems in early childhood as well.

In addition, note that the ECERS and ITERS were used as the comprehensive quality measures in the National Child Care Staffing Study (National Child Care Staffing Study 1989) and the Cost, Quality, and Child Outcomes Study (Helburn 1995), the major studies of their time. The Family Day Care Rating Scale (FDCRS) was used in the Study of Children in Family Child Care and Relative Care (Galinsky, Howes, Kontos, and Shinn 1994). In all of these studies, a relationship was found between higher scores on the rating scales and more positive child development outcomes in areas that are considered important for later school success. The effects of higher quality early childhood experiences have now been shown to last at least through the second grade of elementary school (Peisner-Feinberg, Burchinal, Clifford, Culkin, Howes, Kagan, Yazejian, Byler, Rustici, and Zelazo 1999). Research continues to evaluate longer-lasting effects.

Further, research supports the claim that accreditation impacts quality. As noted in a study by the National Center for the Early Childhood Work Force (1997), "Centers that become NAEYC-accredited demonstrate higher overall classroom quality at the time of embarking on the accreditation process, and show greater improvement in overall quality ratings, staff-child ratios and teacher sensitivity scores" (iv).

So back to the original question: Why pursue a third-party quality endorsement system? Programs offer various reasons for doing so:

- Some are required to pursue endorsement by contract or professional obligations.
- Others live in states that attach ratings and/or dollars to achievement.
- Many parents look for accredited or endorsed programs that assure quality.
- Endorsement can be an important quality assurance and marketing advantage.
- Some pursue endorsement because they feel strongly about support from a third party.
- Others pursue endorsement because they feel the system is a valid tool that helps ensure delivery of high-quality care and education for young children.

Whether any or all of these reasons are your objectives, it is important to clarify and potentially broaden your goals to ensure an optimal experience. What you get out of the experience often depends on the reason(s) you choose to pursue endorsement in the first place. Those guiding objectives will make a difference in your understanding, approach, and emphasis through-out the process.

While most programs serving young children can pursue a quality mea-surement and endorsement system at any time, several characteristics help ensure that a program pursues third-party quality endorsement at a time when it is most likely to succeed. A program doesn't have to be perfect to pursue accreditation from a third-party quality endorsement system. One of the advantages of pursuing a quality endorsement is the process of self-study or evaluation that leads to thoughtful reflection and practice improvement, which should be an expected and welcome part of the experience. Nonetheless, it is helpful to assess the general level of readiness of the program to prepare for the work that lies ahead of you.

Are you ready to pursue a third-party quality endorsement? Complete the assessment in Prove It Activity #1: Are You Ready? to find out. This tool will help you determine your readiness to commit to the process of pursuing a quality measurement and endorsement. If you can answer *yes* to all of the quiz questions you are more than ready to begin. If you say *yes* to most but not all of the questions, make sure you know the answers to the first two quiz questions and then develop a strategic plan to achieve the goals of the remaining questions. You could begin your pursuit now, keeping in mind that you will have additional work to do.

If you answer *no* or *unsure* to most of the questions, it is critical that you carefully evaluate your motivations for pursuing a quality endorsement at this time. You could begin your pursuit now, but be realistic about your timeline, and use all of the self-study tools provided by the third-party quality endorsement system you choose. This will help you make the changes necessary to get to a point where you can respond *yes* to each question on the quiz below. You could also spend time making improvements using this book as a resource before officially beginning your self-study. Either strategy can be effective if you plan it purposefully.

PROVE IT ACTIVITY #1

Are You Ready?

Question	Yes	No	Unsure
Have you determined the primary reasons you are pursuing a third-party quality endorsement?			
Do you have specific outcomes in mind?			
Do you believe your staff and families will support and contribute to the effort?			
Are you willing to honestly assess your program and make necessary changes?			
Are you able to commit the time and finances necessary to succeed?			

Question	Yes	No	Unsure
Is the turnover rate for your administrators and staff relatively stable?			
Is the family-satisfaction rating consistently high?			
Does your program have defined policies and procedures?			
Does your program have an educational philosophy and offer learning opportunities in all domains of early childhood development?			
Does your program consider a high level of health and safety a priority?			
Is your program in good standing with licensing?			
Are your staff members committed to their own professional development, even if it may mean returning to school?			

Now that you have determined your readiness, it is important to find the best system to meet your needs and objectives.

Sunshine Child Development Center

Based on this assessment, Martha feels ready to begin the process. She knows she doesn't have to finish within six months or rush through the process. She simply needs to start considering accreditation criteria as it applies to all activities and personnel at the center. Martha believes this will be an easier way to begin her tenure at the Sunshine Child Development Center rather than having to change a year later.

Choosing a Third-Party Quality Endorsement System

Sunshine Child Development Center

Martha has just completed a meeting at which she introduced the idea of national accreditation more fully to her staff. For the most part they were very receptive, but a few people had questions about which accreditation system they were going to use. Martha acknowledged that she didn't know enough about any of the systems yet but promised to do some research and report back at the next meeting. Martha explained that the center's board had no preference as to which accreditation to pursue, and had left it in her hands to select the one that would best meet the needs of the center, the families, and the children.

This is it! Just like Martha, you have decided to go for it, but you may be unsure which third-party quality endorsement system is right for your program. As mentioned in chapter 1, the early care and education field has many third-party quality endorsement systems to choose from, and selecting the right one for your program can be a daunting task. The early care and education field is expanding rapidly as new research and best practices about the effects of meaningful experiences on young children emerge. This has shaped and reshaped the standards and criteria that third-party quality endorsement systems use to determine what constitutes high-quality care and education. These changes have been most evident in the last few years as state quality rating systems emerge, accreditation systems re-create themselves, and the spotlight is focused on teaching qualifications.

Third-party quality endorsements are no longer just nice to have, but have become a necessity in the life of many programs, particularly if the quality rating systems or child care subsidy agencies use their funding to primarily support accredited centers, as is the case in many states. Additionally, agencies such as National Association of Child Care Resource and Referral Agencies (NACCRRA) often provide most of their fee assistance to families who send their children to accredited centers. In many other cases, state agencies will pay a higher per-child reimbursement to accredited or endorsed centers. This increasingly broad financial reality in our field is one of the motivators for many programs to pursue third-party quality endorsement. When quality endorsement is supported by financial rewards or potentially higher enrollment, many programs are able to reap this second layer of motivation for providing high-quality care and education (the first being that high-quality care and education is good for children in every way).

Another motivator for centers pursuing a third-party quality endorsement is the increased level of family awareness. During the last few years, families have become more educated and interested in what defines high-quality care. Often families do research, ask educated questions, and shop around carefully for the best program they can find for their children. Families expect to see evidence of learning, qualified teachers, an appropriate environment, and other important outcomes of a third-party quality endorsement before enrolling their children. A wealth of information is available to families about what constitutes high-quality care, and one need only search for *child care* on the Internet to find thousands of Web sites and other resources.

As the early care and education field grows, and more home-care through center-care programs become available, third-party quality endorsement has emerged as a way of defining oneself or standing out. Owners, directors, and program administrators are recognizing this benefit and are more often requiring their programs to pursue a quality endorsement. Finally, most states either have or are working on a quality rating system, where an independent third-party quality endorsement, such as accreditation, often rates at the top of the scale. All these factors are motivating programs to seek third-party quality endorsement. The question of whether a program should pursue a third-party quality endorsement is fast becoming moot. What is left is the task of selecting *which* third-party quality endorsement system to pursue.

Getting it right will result in a rich and rewarding self-study that clearly improves the quality of care your program provides. Choosing an endorsement that does not really fit your program's needs will lead your program down a road of frustration and limited success. This chapter will help identify your program's specific needs and match them to the buffet of third-party quality endorsements available at this time. The steps will walk you through how to research endorsements, which questions to ask of whom, and ultimately how to *make a match!*

Occasionally, the senior leadership or governing board of some programs may choose the third-party quality endorsement system. Whether or not this is the case, you will find the steps outlined here useful in helping you understand the scope of the selected endorsement and how it will affect your program.

The quiz in Activity #1 helped you determine one of two answers: *no*, there are areas of opportunity that need to be addressed before you get going; or *yes*, you are ready to begin. If you answered *no*, go to page 35, Prove It Activity #9, Hints and Tips for Getting Ready. If you answered *yes*, read on.

Navigating your way through the choices and offerings described in chapter 1 need not be overwhelming or confusing, especially if you know *why* your program wants this endorsement and *what* each system has to offer.

You can follow three basic steps to make an informed decision about what system will work best for your program to *make a match*.

Step 1: Ask "Why?"

Step 2: Do your homework

Step 3: Make a match!

Step 1: Ask "Why?"

A program may want to pursue a third-party quality endorsement for any number of reasons. You began this work in chapter 1 as you reflected on your program's motivations and readiness. Continuing on, you will investigate further why you are motivated to seek an endorsement at this time. To get started, consider the list of statements below and check as many reasons as are currently relevant to your program.

PROVE IT ACTIVITY #2

Reasons for Pursuing a Third-Party Quality Endorsement

☐ We know we have a high-quality program for children, their families, and our staff, and we want third-party recognition for it.

☐ We want to use a researched set of standards in our effort to increase and maintain quality.

☐ It's a great marketing tool and will increase our enrollment.

☐ It's the next step in our state's quality rating system.

☐ This program can earn additional revenue from the state.

☐ Many families are asking for it.

☐ Many staff members are asking for it.

☐ The governing board/parent forum/executive committee/other senior leadership has decided to pursue a third-party quality endorsement.

☐ It's the next logical step in the growth of quality in this program.

☐ Third-party quality endorsement keeps us on our toes and will ensure we maintain our high standards.

☐ It's good for the children.

☐ It's a personal goal of mine.

☐ Other:

☐ Other:

☐ Other:

- -

It's a good idea to get input from the key stakeholders in your program about their reasons for having your program pursue a third-party quality endorsement. Key stakeholders are any individuals or groups who are invested in the success of your center, including your governing board members, parent forum members, senior or executive leadership, and/or your staff and families. Identify the stakeholders in your program and invite them to share their viewpoints about third-party quality endorsement. Make copies of the checklist from Activity #2 and ask them to complete it. Or create your own list to meet your specific needs.

Once you have collected this information, you will need to summarize it and decide which are your top five reasons for pursuing a third-party quality endorsement. List those top five primary reasons on the next page for easy reference.

☑ PROVE IT ACTIVITY #3

Top Five Reasons for Pursuing a Third-Party Quality Endorsement

Summary of reasons for pursuing a third-party quality endorsement:

1. _____

_____

_____

2. _____

_____

_____

3. _____

_____

_____

4. _____

_____

_____

5. _____

_____

_____

Keep this list handy because you will use it in step 3 when matching your program to an endorsement system.

Step 2: Do Your Homework

In this step you'll do some research about the various third-party quality endorsement systems so that you can select the one that best meets your program's needs and ultimately make a good match in step 3.

First, review your list of reasons and consider whether they generally involve additional revenue, marketing and enrollment, quality, a stakeholder's request, or other priorities. Then investigate further. Once you have determined which reason dominates, go to the corresponding Prove It Activity. For example, if your reason for pursuing a third-party quality endorsement is additional revenue, then complete Prove It Activity #4, Additional Revenue Reasons for Pursuing a Third-Party Quality Endorsement. If your primary reason is marketing and enrollment, complete Prove It Activity #5, Marketing and Enrollment Reasons for Pursuing a Third-Party Quality Endorsement, and so on.

☑ PROVE IT ACTIVITY #4

Additional Revenue Reasons for Pursuing a Third-Party Quality Endorsement

If one of your reasons for pursuing endorsement is that you are interested in earning additional revenue from the state as part of their quality rating system, you will need to contact the state agency managing the QRS (sometimes licensing) and ask a few important questions.

- What are the components and requirements of the state's program?

_____

_____

_____

- Does your program qualify for participation in the state's program?

_____

_____

_____

- What, if any, paperwork do you need to be complete to participate in the state's program?

_____

_____

_____

- Does the state specify which third-party quality endorsements it recognizes in its program?

_____

_____

_____

- Are there any other county or city programs you may qualify for?

_____

_____

_____

- Is there a public awareness piece attached to the state's program? A Web site with ratings? A certificate to hang at your program's location(s)?

_____

_____

_____

Most states have a child care licensing Web site you can access to do your preliminary research. Then contact a representative of the licensing or regulatory agency to ask your questions. This will ensure that you get current information about your state's program. You will use this information in step 3 to help you _make a match._

☑ PROVE IT ACTIVITY #5

Marketing and Enrollment Reasons for Pursuing Third-Party Quality Endorsement

If you identified marketing and enrollment needs as one of your reasons, it is a good idea to find out what other programs in your area are doing. Plot out a twenty-mile radius around your program, and list any programs in this area that you know are similar to yours. If you are a home-based program, look for other home-based programs. If you are a school-age-only program, look for those, and so on. Go to the phone book or Internet and find who is listed and where they are located. Write your findings in the accompanying table.

Center/Program Name	Contact Number	Contact Name	Endorsement
(Example) XYZ Academy	297–555–0098	Anne Brown	NAEYC

Center/Program Name	Contact Number	Contact Name	Endorsement

Call each center or program and speak with the director or administrator to obtain specific information about why they chose the endorsement system they have. Here are some questions to guide you through the conversation:

- How long have you had this endorsement?
- Why did you pick this endorsement system?
- What benefits do you see within your program from having this endorsement?
- What do your families say about this endorsement?
- What does your staff say about this endorsement?
- Would you choose to use this endorsement system again? Why or why not?

If you like, use Researching Your Market in appendix A to make notes about any conversations you have. You will use this information in step 3 to help you *make a match*.

☑ PROVE IT ACTIVITY #6

Quality Reasons for Pursuing a Third-Party Quality Endorsement

If your reasons for pursuing third-party quality endorsement primarily relate to attaining quality, quality improvement, and/or recognition of quality, you need to decide which areas in your program you feel most need to improve or be recognized. Here are a few ideas to get you started:

1. Health and safety
2. Curriculum
3. Interactions
4. Family connections
5. Community connections

6. Teaching staff
7. Administration and general operations
8. The facility or building
9. Relationships/communication
10. Other: _____

To help focus on your program's strengths and opportunities, organize the items in the above list in order with #1 being the strongest, most successful aspect of your program, and #10 being the weakest.

1. _____
2. _____
3. _____
4. _____
5. _____
6. _____
7. _____
8. _____
9. _____
10. _____

You will use this list in step 3 to help you *make a match*.

✔ PROVE IT ACTIVITY #7

Key Stakeholders' Requests as Reasons for Pursuing a Third-Party Quality Endorsement

If stakeholders, families, and/or staff have asked for a third-party quality endorsement, find out why. We recommend you use the list of reasons in Activity #2 to help you make this determination. Typically you will hear one or more reasons such as seeking additional state revenue, marketing and enrollment, or service and operational quality. If this is the case, go back to the previous pages and complete Activities #4, #5, or #6.

✔ PROVE IT ACTIVITY #8

Other Reasons for Pursuing a Third-Party Quality Endorsement

If you are seeking a third-party quality endorsement for any other reasons, it is important that you and the key stakeholders examine these reasons. We recommend you use the list of reasons in Activity #2 to help you make this examination.

Step 3: Make a Match!

The final step in the decision-making process involves getting acquainted with the available third-party quality endorsement systems. You will use the information collected in Step 2 to help with this research.

Make a Match for Additional Revenue

If your match is driven by seeking out additional revenue from the state, then your options are limited to the third-party quality endorsement systems recognized in your state's program.

Your next step will be to research some specific information about these third-party quality endorsement systems. The Third-Party Quality Endorsement System Information form in appendix A can help you with this task. After you have gathered all this information, take time to reflect on and compare it. Lay the sheets side by side and compare the characteristics of each third-party quality endorsement system. Be sure to consider the factors on the worksheet that have the greatest impact on your program. For example, how much can your budget support? What are your teachers' current qualifications? Are staff members prepared to further their professional development? Does your program meet the state's licensing requirements? By examining these questions, you should be able to determine which third-party quality endorsement will work best for you.

Congratulations, you have made a match!

Hint: If your program was assigned to a third-party quality endorsement system, you can use the Third-Party Quality Endorsement Information form in appendix A to help you become more familiar with some of the components and requirements of that system.

Make a Match for Marketing and Enrollment

If your match is driven by marketing and enrollment needs, then you should base your decision on whatever third-party quality endorsement system is best-known and successful in your area. Use the information you collected in step 2 to identify these endorsement systems, and then go to Third-Party Quality Endorsement System Information in appendix A to do further research.

After gathering all this information, lay the sheets side by side and compare the characteristics of each third-party quality endorsement system. Be sure to consider the factors on the worksheet that match the needs of your program. For example, does the main focus of the third-party quality endorsement system match the strengths in your program? Will this system help your program improve its weakest areas? Answers to these questions will help you determine which third-party quality endorsement system will work best for your program.

Congratulations, you have made a match!

Make a Match for Quality

If your match is driven by attaining quality, quality improvement, and/or recognition of quality, then you have many options for a third-party quality endorsement system. Picking the appropriate one will largely depend on your program's current and potential strengths. Go back to the list you created in Activity #6 to review them.

The next step is to do some research about what is available to you. To start, review the list of third-party quality endorsement systems beginning on page 14. It is by no means a complete list, and we encourage you to dig deeper. Use the Third-Party Quality Endorsement System Information worksheet in appendix A to record the information you collect. Then compare the characteristics of each third-party quality endorsement system. Take into consideration the factors on the worksheet that match the needs of your program. For example, does the third-party quality endorsement system match the strengths in your program? Will this third-party quality endorsement help your program improve in the weakest areas? Answering these questions will help you to determine which third-party quality endorsement will work best for you.

Congratulations, you have made a match!

If you answered *no*—there are areas of opportunity that need to be addressed before you move on to Activity #2—read on.

✓ PROVE IT ACTIVITY #9

Hints and Tips for Getting Ready

If your program answered mostly *no* to questions in the Activity #1 assessment, but you are still eager and motivated to start the process toward quality improvement and endorsement, then follow along for some helpful hints and tips to help you get ready.

Refer back to your answers to Activity #1. You will use them to complete the table that follows. Next to each question are suggestions on how to drive your program closer to being able to answer *yes* to all the questions in the quiz.

No Answers to the Are You Ready? Quiz

Check all the questions to which you answered *no* in the Are You Ready? assessment:

No	Assessment Question	Improvement Suggestion
	Have you determined the primary reasons you are pursuing a third-party quality endorsement?	You and your key stakeholders need to examine these reasons. To help you do so, we recommend using the list of questions in Activity #2: Reasons for Pursuing a Third-Party Quality Endorsement.
	Do you have specific outcomes in mind?	Meet with your key stakeholders and discuss what the program wants to achieve by pursuing a third-party quality endorsement, for example, assurance of quality for parents or a higher rating in the state QRS. After determining these outcomes, program management should put a plan of action in place to align the program with these outcomes.
	Do you believe your staff and families will support and contribute to the effort?	Any third-party quality endorsement will require the full participation of your program's staff and enrolled families. It is essential to find out what level of commitment you can expect. A good way to do this is to review other projects your program has undertaken in the past; examine what you did to ensure participation, and whether these things can be duplicated.

No	Assessment Question	Improvement Suggestion
	Are you willing to honestly assess your program and make necessary changes?	The most important first step toward program improvement is to examine and honestly review areas of opportunity. It can be a difficult process because you will need to recognize where your program falls short. But ultimately, an honest and in-depth look will make for a more successful self-study.
	Are you able to commit the time and finances necessary to succeed?	Ideally, third-party quality endorsement should be built into an annual budget, not decided upon on the spur of the moment. Costs involved not only include the endorsement materials and tools, but also the overall investment the program must make in its facilities, resources, and staff training. Just like finances, you'll need to allocate (and budget) time for the self-study to be done correctly. Money and time must be considered in tandem with the other reasons your program is pursuing this endorsement.
	Is the turnover rate for your administrators and staff relatively stable?	High turnover of teaching staff and management will not positively contribute to the overall success of your program, and definitely not to a third-party quality endorsement project. Before starting the endorsement process, a center director should ideally be in place for a minimum of six months. This is a minimum time frame that could also be applied to the program's lead teaching staff. Although these time frames are not currently mandatory for all third-party quality endorsement systems, they are strongly and increasingly recommended.
	Is the family-satisfaction rating consistently high?	Although most third-party quality endorsements require a survey of the families, it is a good idea to ensure you have achieved a high rate of family satisfaction before submitting for endorsement. As a general rule, seeking third-party quality endorsement should be motivated by the fact that you *already* have a moderate to high level of quality in your program. If you do not, this should be a priority as you work on improvements throughout the self-study or before you even begin. Go back to chapter 1 and review the section What Is a Third-Party Quality Endorsement System? that talks about the three levels of quality within a program.
	Does your program have defined policies and procedures?	This is an important part of showing evidence to the third-party quality endorser. Having written policies available for review by the families and staff in your program ensures equity and consistency for all families and staff. Some endorsement systems make exceptions in specific situations. If there are any questions, contact them directly. See Developing Policies and Procedures in appendix C for more tips.

No	Assessment Question	Improvement Suggestion
	Does your program have an educational philosophy and offer learning opportunities in all domains of early childhood development?	This is an integral part of any program as part of showing evidence to the third-party quality endorsement system. The program philosophy should to be written, evident in your classrooms, and available for review by the families and the staff in your program.
	Does your program consider a high level of health and safety a priority?	All states have minimum licensing standards for child care programs. Review your licensing records to determine your program's history of meeting these standards, particularly those involving health and safety. A program should have a clean licensing record, especially in this area, before attempting third-party quality endorsement.
	Is your program in good standing with licensing?	All third-party endorsements require this. Programs having a temporary, suspended, or probationary license need to be relicensed before pursuing third-party quality endorsement.
	Are your staff members committed to their own professional development, even if it may mean returning to school?	An essential part of achieving a third-party quality endorsement involves professional development for your teaching staff. You need to work with your staff to create appropriate professional development plans that meet both their needs as well as those of your program.

Your Role as the Leader

Sunshine Child Development Center

Martha has done her research and made the important decision to pursue NAC accreditation. It is recognized by her state, and after careful research, she feels it is the best fit for her program. She is confident that NAC will help her ensure high quality in her program. Now she just has to get her staff on board. As a newer director she is still working to gain their trust and confidence. Staff members are happy with things the way they are, so Martha is unsure how to bring them together to achieve accreditation. Martha knows what her goals are, but has to understand her role as a leader in the process before she can succeed.

Congratulations! You've accomplished a lot to reach this point. It is a significant step to choose and commit to a specific third-party quality endorsement system, and not unlike other major commitments in life, such as signing your first lease on an apartment or buying your first car or house. Often people are both happy and nervous at the same time, wondering what they have gotten themselves into but eager to find out. Once the decision has been made, it is instinct to jump right in, get things started, begin completing paperwork, meet requirements, and so on. However, it is typically more advantageous to first spend time researching and planning. Embarking on a journey that will take, at minimum, the better part of a year deserves forethought. But many people skip this vital step for various reasons:

- Childhood educators working in the field are doers; they are accustomed to constant action and movement.
- No defined support tools embedded in any of the third-party quality endorsement systems require, or even support, a preplanning phase.
- Being hands-on is more comfortable for many people.
- The leaders are new or inexperienced in directing a team through a strategic process such as this.

This journey should not be taken lightly. As the leader, you must prepare yourself not only to understand the system you have chosen but also to understand how to support and communicate with your staff as they learn, grow, develop, and change. While you can share this charge with an assistant director or other support staff, *you* must be the guide and the person in charge (to meet criteria and to achieve the highest level of success and quality) on this journey.

How Adults Learn

Understanding how adults learn while going through this process is like having a magic trick in your back pocket. Adults differ significantly from children in how and why they learn. In an early care and education setting, we are focused primarily on the children's learning, and rightly so. However, the teachers in our programs should also be constantly learning and evolving as professionals and they will often rely on you, their leader, to help them accomplish that. It can only help your professional relationship as you go through a momentous experience, such as accreditation, to be able to teach, mentor, and guide the teachers in your program so they can fully benefit from the experience and pass that on as they teach children. Many resources are available on how adults learn and how to teach adults. We won't pretend that our discussion is inclusive; however, a few basic principles will help you shape your approach toward leading your teachers through this process.

Many sources list characteristics of adult learning. An inclusive but concise list of characteristics can be found in the American Society for Training and Development *ASTD Training Certification Manual* (Biech and West 2004). Another good source for understanding adult's learning needs is *Best Practices for Training Early Childhood Professionals* by Sharon Bergen (2009).

Adults Learn Because They Are Motivated

Children may want or have to learn, but they also just learn because it's all new, all a discovery. They are often unable to rationally decide what they should learn or how they might apply that knowledge. They constantly absorb information, make connections, and assimilate details as they go. As adults, we make choices about what new information or experiences we are going to let in. Surely there is a level of subconscious learning that occurs, but if we don't have a motivation, information often does not move into long-term memory.

Adults Have Different Learning Styles

It is important to understand how individual teachers learn best. Are they kinesthetic, visual, or auditory learners? In the same vein, it is also important for you to know how you learn best. Teachers, trainers, coaches, and so on often share information with others in the style they prefer, which can unfortunately alienate some of their learners. If you are an auditory learner you might tend toward talking things out, lecturing, and using other verbal methods. In that case, your visual learners will get lost or forget what you've said unless you provide a handout or diagram to support your message. Taking learning style quizzes and discussing their results could be a bonding and insightful activity for you and your staff.

Refer to the Learning Styles Quiz in appendix A for an example you can use with your staff.

Adults Learn Best in an Informal Atmosphere

This seems like a commonsense statement but often leaders overly formalize their messages, whether in memos or staff meetings or even books (not this one, of course!). Granted, sometimes the topic may require a certain level of formality, but the atmosphere should be one of comfort for adults and respect—a place where ideas can be shared and heard, where frustrations can be acknowledged and team efforts toward solutions are encouraged, and where accomplishments are celebrated and laughter is welcome.

Adults Learn Best When Practical Application Is Encouraged

You can tell a person all day long how to install a garage door opener but if she doesn't have an immediate use for this information, she will likely not care much about what she is learning or allow it to take up space in her precious long-term memory. It is critical that you support the connections between information sharing and practical application. For example, if you introduce a new head-count system in your program, you should immediately practice it via role-play or simulation. Then in the days following, observe the teachers to ensure they are held accountable for the information. This will encourage application, which cements learning.

Adults See Themselves as Self-Directed and Responsible

You may have noticed the statement in the preceding paragraph, "It is critical that you *support* the connections . . ." We carefully worded this statement to ensure the message is not, "It is critical that you *make* the connections . . ." Adults need to be respected as learners. As a leader, you function as a guide, not a hand-holder. Adults will tune out if they feel you don't respect their ability to participate in their own learning. The following proverb sums up this principle: "Tell me and I'll forget. Show me and I may remember. Involve me and I'll learn."

Adults Bring a Wealth of Experience to the Learning Environment

This principle relates nicely to the first one mentioned. In early care and education, we are accustomed to our learners having little experience to draw on, and we celebrate those first connections with prior knowledge as significant cognitive developments. But adults do this without even thinking. Prior knowledge and experience affect all new learning and experiences for adults and can be more valuable than anything you may share with them. Leaders are also learners, and allowing other adults to share their expertise will strengthen everyone's learning.

Adults Learn Best When They Can Relate Learning to What They Know

Think of your brain as a wall of mailboxes in a high-rise apartment building. There are many, many slots, each labeled with a different topic. As adults learn new information, they subconsciously put the information in a relevant mailbox, attaching it to already-known information. This increases the information's impact. If adult learners can't find a mailbox for the information you are providing, their brains either create a new one or toss out the information. If they go through the work of creating a new mailbox but don't immediately use the information, the information will be weakly stored because it has yet to have relevance or meaning. This analogy is an example of the principle in action: you are learning this principle by connecting it to something you already know—mailboxes. If you can ensure that the new learning you introduce has a clear connection to prior knowledge, it will make a stronger impact.

Adults Have Ideas to Contribute

Adults are motivated to be part of their learning, and they have prior knowledge and experience to share. They also have ideas. New ideas should be revered, not because they will all be implemented, but because creativity and idea generation should be valued. This value, common to optimal learning environments, will help adults shine; ideas will flow freely, and then, who knows what could happen? That environment may be the birthplace of your program's next great idea.

These principles hold true whether you are conducting a staff meeting, introducing a new curriculum or teaching strategy, or embarking on a third-party quality endorsement system. Consider the principles carefully as you take each step in a third-party quality endorsement process, and your results will no doubt be enhanced.

Beyond understanding how adults learn, using effective communication skills and practices is essential. Communication skills such as delegation are invaluable leadership strategies you can use throughout the process, and it is important to implement those tools effectively.

Communicating Effectively in Your Program

Communication is an essential tool available to you. What, when, and how you communicate with your staff members will directly impact your success. Communication is often confused with talking. We talk all day long, but good communication involves thought and practice. Communication is a two-way street—whether the communication is written or verbal, there should be opportunity for one person to "talk" and the other to listen and then "respond," continuing in a cyclical fashion. Effective communication involves mutual trust and honesty, concise language, clear expectations, and continual follow-up until resolution. Consider the following two examples and determine which follows the guidelines for effective communication.

Example 1

Patrice, maybe it's me. I'm not sure, but I can't believe how behind you are on your classroom observations. I guess you're not part of the team. Natalie told me that last week when she asked for help, you just shrugged at her. What is that all about?

Example 2

Hi, Patrice. I need to speak with you. I just checked on the status of the classroom observations. I see yours are not complete, and the deadline has passed. I want to be sure I understand what is preventing you from meeting this deadline so we can resolve this in the best way for both of us.

Clearly, the second example sets a safe tone, but also clear expectations, including an expectation of resolution. The first example is riddled with poor communication: sarcasm, third-person messages, blaming self to avoid confrontation, and so on. The conversations you engage in with your staff will sometimes be similar to these exchanges, but if your overall communication is done well, many confrontations can be avoided.

Being a skilled listener is also important. We tend to focus on the message we want to get across instead of on what the other person is saying. Being an active listener by doing things such as paraphrasing, reflecting, using receptive body language, and refraining from interrupting are often challenging but will exponentially increase the effectiveness of your communication with others (University of Maryland 2008).

Planned and purposeful communication strategies will save you from the many common and disruptive pitfalls. Let's talk further about some specific ways to use communication.

Motivation

If your teachers are not already intrinsically motivated to achieve the third-party quality endorsement, they will need to find motivation elsewhere. You can play a big role in providing and maintaining such motivation. In this case, adults are similar to children—positive reinforcement, celebrating small achievements, and practical application go a long way in encouraging motivation in adults.

✔ PROVE IT SUGGESTIONS

Motivation

- Ask your staff to write down a few reasons about why they work with children and/or what impact they'd like to have on children's lives. Then clearly outline for staff the benefits of the third-party quality endorsement system for the children. Make the connection between their goals and the benefits of a third-party quality endorsement system.

- Break the tasks for quality improvement into smaller parts, and celebrate achievements along the way rather than waiting until the final achievement. For example, ice cream sundaes when all observations are complete, an extra ten-minute break per person when everyone completes their document collection, and so on.
- Brag about your teachers within their earshot. Tell current and prospective families about the process you are going through, and let them know how the teachers are contributing.
- Share data about other programs in the area that have the third-party quality endorsement system you are pursuing. Odds are you may be one of the few pursuing this endorsement (or receiving it, if this is a reaccreditation).
- Create a timeline, map, thermometer, or other gauge on posterboard to visually track progress so it is measured and an end is in sight.
- Get your hands dirty. Work as hard as you ask others to work, and they will be more motivated to work along side you.
- Set high expectations, and keep them high, knowing part of your role is to help staff reach those goals. Many will not achieve your expectations fully, so the higher (yet still realistic) you set them, the higher your staff will reach in an effort to meet them.
- Say *thank you*—and mean it—every chance you get it. You can't do this alone.

Delegation

Many a strong center director falls short when delegating. For many reasons, people avoid delegation. Perhaps we feel we are imposing or passing off work that should be ours. We often try to avoid conflicts, and assigning tasks to those who may not want them seems like a way to start an argument. But the more practical and realistic way to look at delegation is that, if done right, it is a way to show your staff members respect. Additionally, it helps them grow professionally. A teacher may find she is interested in becoming a center director after helping with a family event. Another teacher may develop his organizational and time-management skills if he is tasked with assembling documentation to meet criteria. Remember—*adults see themselves as self-directed and responsible.* Delegating tasks sends a message that you consider your staff responsible and a team. The Prove It Suggestions that follow offer easy ways to begin and sustain a culture in your center that supports delegation and a team environment.

✓ PROVE IT SUGGESTIONS

Delegation

- Delegate something to everybody. Leaving some people out will make it seem as though you are playing favorites or judging abilities.
- Purposefully decide what you can delegate. Make a list of things others can help with.
- Check progress regularly and alter assignments as needed. Delegating does not mean you are giving up all responsibility for the task and it doesn't mean the delegate will excel at the task right away.
- The people you are delegating to need to feel trusted and respected to succeed. Do not delegate anything you have a specific vision for and do not stand over anyone's shoulder once you've shared instructions.
- If you are having a hard time thinking of things to delegate, ask for ideas at a staff meeting. Simply tell your staff "I need help with some tasks. I am going to assign small tasks to each person that will help our program become stronger and help us work better as a team. Please write down three things you'd be willing to help with."

Coaching

As the program administrator or center director you are more than a boss or supervisor; you are a leader and a coach. Whether they realize it or not, your staff looks to you for development and guidance. Thinking of yourself as a coach will help you define your role, especially as you proceed through a third-party quality endorsement system, potentially a time of tremendous growth and learning for both you and your staff. Using already-researched and developed standards of excellence to measure your current practices is an excellent way to increase your knowledge, skills, and abilities, and those of the teachers in your program. Conversely, if the third-party quality endorsement system is seen only as something you must endure, you and your staff will likely miss all of the professional development benefits embedded in the third-party quality endorsement system. Understanding your role as a coach and the benefits of the third-party quality endorsement system will optimize your chances at success and the care and learning you provide for children. A coach

- guides others to find the answers themselves versus telling them what to do;
- assesses each individual's skills, talents, and opportunities;
- focuses efforts toward meeting established goals;
- provides feedback about areas of success and areas of opportunity and a plan to work on those areas and follow up at a predetermined time;
- doesn't avoid something because it is difficult;
- often pushes people to achieve as a team more than they could have achieved alone.

Instituting a Culture of Change in Your Program

Any leader about to embark on a changing process needs to understand elements of change management, including barriers and methods to overcome them.

"A change is coming." What feelings does that phrase provoke in you? For some, the phrase elicits feelings of anticipation, excitement, curiosity, motivation, and the like. For many others, it arouses feelings of trepidation, anxiety, and worry. Often the word *change* is associated with negativity although we know that is not always true; change can be very positive, such as a new baby, a wedding, a job promotion, a new house, or achievement of a third-party quality endorsement system. However, knowing all this, it is essential to prepare for the feelings and resistance you might encounter in your program and teachers. The skills needed to adapt and respond positively to change contribute to many aspects of job success and satisfaction and are skills your staff will be fortunate to learn with your help.

Additionally, always consider the variety of experience, skills, and knowledge your teachers have to share. Your team can help one another in all steps of this process by sharing their strengths and overcoming their weaknesses. Responding and adapting to change is no different. Some of your teachers will have experienced much change and it may or may not have been positive; others may have encountered very little change in their careers. Either way, it takes a leader armed with knowledge and skills to guide them effectively.

The director's role is significant in this process. Not only does the director lead the program through the process of achieving a third-party quality endorsement—essentially a change process—but the director's actions and attitudes serve as a model for the teachers and families in the program. If the director is positive, enthusiastic, and purposeful in her actions, many of the worries felt by others may dissolve without much effort.

Before you are expected to model a positive attitude toward change, it is essential to evaluate your *actual* attitude.

 **PROVE IT ACTIVITY #10**

My Attitude toward Change

Evaluate your attitude toward change by placing a check mark in the appropriate column to indicate your gut reaction to each situation.

Situation	Bring it on 5	Okay 4	So-so 3	A little nervous 2	Sweaty palms 1
You and a good friend have plans for the weekend. You have had these plans for two weeks. She calls Friday afternoon and suggests a change to the plans.					
You have hired a new teacher for the infant classroom but the day before she is supposed to start she asks to work in the preschool classroom where you have an opening as well.					
Your boss tells you that for training purposes, your assistant director is trading places with an assistant director at a nearby program for two weeks.					
You go to a salon or barbershop. Your normal stylist is out sick, and a brand-new stylist is assigned to cut your hair. She suggests a shorter length.					
You go to your favorite restaurant only to notice the menu has changed. A brand-new, talented chef is now in charge, but all your favorites have been replaced.					
You have been managing a program for three years. You have worked hard daily to ensure that children, families, and staff have good experiences in your program. At a board meeting, you are informed that you are expected to pursue a third-party quality endorsement system.					

Total your points for all situations.

IF YOU SCORED BETWEEN 25 AND 30, YOU ARE EAGER AND READY FOR CHANGE.

Your program will truly benefit from your willingness to adapt and take on new things with zeal. Be cautious, however; your comfort with change might make you a bit of a change-aholic and you don't want to scare others with your zest for the new and different.

IF YOU SCORED BETWEEN 18 AND 24, YOU ARE CAUTIOUSLY OPTIMISTIC ABOUT CHANGE.

You possess a positive attitude toward change mixed with a healthy dose of caution. It is important to consider each change independently before forming an attitude toward it. Because of this balanced approach, be aware of the possibility of appearing too neutral about change to others. A positive outward approach is important for a leader to demonstrate.

IF YOU SCORED BETWEEN 9 AND 17, YOU ARE COMFORTABLE WITH THE PREDICTABLE.

You typically shy away from change and usually stay with what makes you most comfortable. However, with good reason and time to adjust, you are willing to change and can embrace new direction wholeheartedly if you understand the benefits of doing so. You may seem defensive to others when a change is suggested and you hesitate. Be cautious of your initial reactions. Being careful and considerate of each potential change is completely acceptable, but as the leader it is important that your hesitation not be seen as fear or doubt.

IF YOU SCORED 8 OR LESS, YOU ARE CHANGE-PHOBIC.

You get up at the same time each day, have the same thing for breakfast, and go to work at the same time, and it has been working for you just fine, thank you very much. Change often seems more work than it is worth and you are often skeptical and stubborn about new changes that come along. While that can often be a fair perspective based on experience, you need to put your personal feelings aside when leading staff members. They gauge their reaction to changes and initiatives based on your reaction. By avoiding and disregarding potential opportunities for change, you may be inhibiting your staff.

Adopting Practices for Change

Now that you know how you personally approach change, it is important for you as a leader to adopt a few habits or practices that encourage an effective approach toward change:

- Understand your intended outcome, that is, your vision.
- Practice articulating your vision and explaining why it is your vision—in writing, out loud, or any other way that will help you share it confidently with others.
- Develop a plan with incremental and achievable steps.
- Avoid setting a false expectation that maintaining the status quo is acceptable.
- Embrace the positive qualities of change and share them with others. Don't *sell* them, *share* them.
- Treat teachers as professionals. All professional fields encounter change on a consistent basis.

Tips for Instituting a Culture of Change

As a leader, first ensure that *you* are informed and prepared so you can effectively lead. Then focus on how you share your information and vision so those you lead will be eager to follow. The culture and atmosphere you develop in your center will be instrumental in this effort.

 **PROVE IT SUGGESTIONS**

Instituting a Culture of Change

- Meet change head on. Have a staff meeting focused on change, allow all staff to take the assessment in Activity #10, and openly discuss feelings about change.
- Provide a framework of reference. Evaluate changes that have already occurred that were successful with positive outcomes.
- Use positive reinforcement: reward teachers with small prizes, such as notepads, fun teacher supplies, or treats, whenever they institute a change for the better in their classrooms, practice improved teaching methods, pursue professional development, and so on. Pay careful attention to different teachers' comfort levels. For example, a

teacher who does not do well with change should get a lot of positive reinforcement at first, more so than a teacher who seeks change.

- Have a "Suggestions for Positive Change" box and encourage staff to contribute ideas to it.
- Explain why change is necessary and desirable.
- Involve others when appropriate. Then instead of change always happening to them, sometimes change is happening because of them.
- Communicate, communicate, communicate.

Setting goals and planning incremental steps are important actions to ensure that change occurs. Action-planning tools will be discussed more thoroughly in later chapters, but those same tools are relevant when planning any kind of action or change.

Sunshine Child Development Center

Wow! Being a leader is an important responsibility. But equipped with the right tools and knowledge, it seems easier than just telling people what to do. Martha realizes that knowing how to support her staff is as important as knowing how to support children. She is committed to maintaining an open, collaborative, and individualized relationship with each staff member. While a small amount of resistance and trepidation still remains among the team members, Martha's approach is putting them at ease and most are willing to put their best effort into the accreditation process.

Professional Development

Sunshine Child Development Center

Martha is excited to begin introducing the NAC system to her staff and families. The more she has learned about the process of accreditation, the more enthusiastic she has become. However, one thing worries her. She is concerned about her staff's reaction to an increase in professional development expectations. A few of her staff members have a degree or certification—either an associate's or bachelor's degree or a child development associate (CDA) credential—but for the most part they all have met only the minimum qualifications set forth by the state. In addition, the previous center management had not developed systems for staff to pursue their state required in-service hours in a systematic way, leading to a culture that doesn't value professional development opportunities. Martha feels strongly that to succeed and meet the true intent of the standards she will have to help her staff understand the value of pursuing continued professional development. She herself has an associate's degree in child development and is considering pursuing further education. Each time she has broached the topic in the past, staff members have answered her warily with reasons why they can't pursue further professional development, usually involving time and money. Martha determines she must develop a plan to help them overcome these barriers if she wants her program to reap the highest rewards of third-party quality endorsement.

Background and Research on Professional Development

There is always a reaction, from one extreme or the other, when discussing the topic of professional development in relation to a third-party quality endorsement system. Often the first assumption is that professional development means formal education, even though professional development encompasses much more. Some people think the additional education recommendations are one of the most important progressive moves our field has made in many years. They firmly believe the research correlates higher levels of teacher education with increased positive outcomes for children.

There are also many who feel that teacher education levels alone do not dictate the quality of care for children, and that we may be doing more harm than good by focusing so strongly on education levels for early childhood education (ECE) teachers that are not in line with the current workforce. People in this camp often cite statistics affirming the positive outcomes of many children taught by well-trained and highly experienced teachers having low levels of formal education. In between, of course, are a million and one variations of these opinions.

What most of us seem to agree on is that professional development—whether composed simply of staff meetings or in-service hours, earned with or without continuing education units (CEUs), or formal education from the child development associate to master's degree level—is essential. Professional development keeps the knowledge of those working directly with children current and sharp and infuses their teaching practices with enthusiasm, motivation, and purpose.

Unfortunately, the "most of us" referred to in the previous paragraph is typically a collection of program administrators, researchers, consultants, owners, and managers. Early childhood teachers too often are not part of this group. Of course, it is impossible to make generalizations in this scenario, and we are not attempting to do so. With their differing backgrounds, educational philosophies, levels of education, and work environments, teachers' opinions are as varied as everyone else's on this topic.

Current industry workforce statistics from the Economic Policy Institute's report *Losing Ground in Early Childhood Education* (Herzenberg, Price, and Bradley 2005) can tell us a lot. According to the report, 30 percent of center teachers had formal degrees in 2004 compared with 43 percent in 1983. Teachers do not always embrace or seek formal education or professional development, especially if they lack motivation. Perhaps they haven't perceived a strong "bang for their buck" in past professional development opportunities. Or maybe they feel a strain on resources such as time and money. The long-term benefits to the children in their care are not often implicit and the personal short- or long-term advantages are also not apparent. As we know from research on adult learning discussed in the previous chapter, this lack of connection is a critical error in current professional development opportunities for ECE teachers.

Unfortunately, many of us who spend our time, energy, and passion focused on ECE consider ourselves professionals, but many onlookers (and even a few insiders) view us as just doing a job on par with babysitting or another entry-level service position. Therefore, as a leader you have two important roles: One role is to provide professional development opportunities, potentially including acquisition of higher levels of education, and to mentor, model, and maybe even help edit homework—all of which are critically important. The second role is to help teachers—those who need the help—understand the importance of seeking and valuing higher levels of professional development.

Because of the unique situation in which ECE professionals find themselves, it is sometimes hard for teachers to understand what is "in it" for them. They might wonder why an all-day Saturday class is worth their time and effort and how it will have a positive impact on their work. Even more significantly, they might wonder why seeking a four-year degree while also working full time is a worthwhile goal. Consider these analogies to help you explain that value to teachers.

Analogy 1

Your family doctor recommends you see a specialist. He has two you can choose from. The first is a recently graduated doctor who has just been trained in all that modern medicine has to offer. The second has been practicing for twenty years and graduated at the top of her class in 1988. However, she has skipped all classes, briefings, seminars, and so on related to new research in her field since she graduated. Which doctor would you choose?

Typically, those who are asked this question don't like either option. They want a specialist with a combination of experience, education, and ongoing professional development. While the pay level is clearly different for doctors and early childhood educators, the importance of the role is similar. Early childhood educators could consider their services—their craft—on par with that of physicians practicing preventative medicine. Their students, and the parents of their students, should want the same dedication to ongoing growth and development from both professions.

Analogy 2

You need to get in touch with a friend. You sit down at your typewriter with your trusty bottle of white correction fluid. You type your letter and then go to the post office to send the letter overnight since you need your friend to receive the letter right away. Many people have suggested you get a computer and use e-mail but you have decided that nothing new in the past twenty-five years could possibly improve your life. You also go to the bank every time you need cash because you won't use ATMs, you only drive cars with roll-down windows and press-down locks, you walk across the room to change the channel on the television . . .

At this point listeners are often shaking their heads, feeling sympathy for the poor soul whose life is so hard because she refuses to change and adapt. Simply equating the goal of recommended professional development in third-party quality endorsement systems to this scenario and asking teachers to consider ensuring that their knowledge and skills are updated to reflect current practice often illuminates the reasons for doing so.

The reality is that most current third-party quality endorsement systems include some element related to professional development. This is true of established systems and those currently in development. Because part of the goal of pursuing a third-party quality endorsement is to ensure the care and education you provide is the best of the best, teachers and administrators alike must be willing to work on how they *prepare to practice* and not just how they actually practice. As the second analogy suggests, refusing to update and learn new things can be downright silly. It doesn't mean throwing out old knowledge—it means incorporating innovation and new research. As professional educators, it is even sillier to object or resist, especially when we have such ability to affect and shape the lives of children. That doesn't mean learning new things will be easy, but it is a logical next step.

Current Situation and Expectations

The National Association for the Education of Young Children (NAEYC) was the first accreditation organization to set mandatory requirements for staff qualifications (in their candidacy requirements). Many endorsement systems have been grappling with the issue of professional development in the past few years. Currently, almost all third-party quality endorsement systems have begun incorporating professional development recommendations and/or requirements in their criteria. For example, NAC recommends that teachers have a CDA or equivalent and two years of teaching experience. NAEYC's candidacy requirements state that 75 percent of teachers have a minimum of a CDA or equivalent (defined by NAEYC) or other college experiences (defined by NAEYC in candidacy requirements).

Nevertheless, these goals are often not reflective of the current work-force. According to the Center for the Child Care Work Force (2002), only 33 percent of center teachers have a bachelor's degree and another 47 percent have had some college-level work, which may or may not be in early child-hood education. Affecting all of this is the fact that many states do not require any specialized training (beyond a high school diploma) to work as an ECE teacher (National Association for Regulatory Administration and the National Child Care Information and Technical Assistance Center 2005).

This situation is slowly changing as the increased focus on teacher quali-fications is making an impact. More and more states now consider a CDA a basic qualification for teachers. But if a program requires a higher level of education, it often has to pay higher wages; those costs are passed on to par-ents and, therefore, could potentially price child care out of the market.

In a society where value is often determined by money, it is no wonder that the general population doesn't value the ECE profession as much as it does other equally important occupations. The pay is typically low, indicating (incorrectly) that the work is less valuable. Attracting and retaining teachers with higher levels of education becomes quite challenging.

How to Achieve Staff Qualification Requirements

The concept of "it is what it is" seems appropriate here. The professional development climate in ECE is muddled right now, to say the least, but we still have to work in it—not only work but thrive. So how do we do that? The best place to start is with the culture and expectations you establish in your program for staff. As their leader, you set the tone and model attitudes and approaches. If you value professional development *and* positively reinforce staff as they pursue, achieve, and apply new learning, you will establish a culture of lifelong learning in no time. If you apologize to staff for making them work after hours or help them find easy solutions, you will perpetuate a culture that does not value development. As illustrated in the analogies on pages 53–54, ECE teachers must be treated as professionals. Embracing pro-fessional development is an ideal opportunity to do that. Just as we encourage learning for children, we should do the same for adults by respecting their need for growth, development, and discovery.

Before requiring something of your staff, develop the best plan for getting there. To do so, you first need to understand where they have been.

In-Service and Professional Development Hours

Many state licensing agencies have some requirement for in-service or professional development hours. Ask yourself the following questions:

- What are our state's requirements for professional development?
- Do I feel the state's requirements are adequate? If not, what do I feel is adequate?
- Have staff been expected to meet those requirements in the past? If yes, how?
- What has been the most successful method for meeting requirements and gaining quality information or skills?
- Do staff meetings count as training? Do training hours need to be CEUs?
- What resources do I have to help my staff meet the required number of training hours?
- What are the preferred learning methods of each staff member?
- What type of professional development is appropriate for each staff member?
- Does the state require that trainers or providers of in-service hours be state-approved?

To help answer a few of these questions, develop a chart something like this one:

In-Service and Professional Development Planning Chart

Name	State (or Program) Requirement	Preferred Method	Plan for Achieving	Status
Julio	40 hours	Attend full-day workshops	May 10, 8 hr. "Creativity in the Classroom"	20 hours as of May 30
Renate	40 hours	Child Care Exchange CEU courses	Will review offerings and choose	5 hours as of May 30
Jessica	20 hours	Attend evening courses or online resource and referral offerings	Register for 3 evening courses, attend a local AEYC conference	1 course complete by May 30
Mizuki	20 hours	Attend workshops, any time	Contact resource and referral	No hours completed

See In-Service and Professional Development Planning Chart in appendix A for a blank version of this chart.

Answering these questions and recording the answers on this chart will help you establish your goals. The preferred means by which your staff members seek professional development should not be the only way they experience professional development. However, knowing and acknowledging their preferences can motivate staff by helping them feel they are part of the process versus simply fulfilling a requirement and will encourage them to attain higher levels of learning and application.

RESOURCES

One of the challenges is finding high-quality resources for in-service training. States may to some degree regulate the type of in-service hours that are accepted. You need to educate yourself on these requirements and always be cognizant of them when making decisions about hours. Listed below are a few resources for in-service hours:

- *Exchange Magazine*—beginning workshops
- Child Care Exchange Web site www.childcareexchange.com
- Zero to Three training and conferences
- National Association of Child Care Professionals (NACCP) online training programs
- Applebaum training seminars
- Local Association for the Education of Young Children (AEYC) affiliate/conferences
- Local Child Care Association (CCA) conferences
- National conferences such as NAEYC or NACCP
- Local resource and referral agencies
- Local YMCA
- Noncredit courses at local colleges or vocational-technical schools
- For-credit courses at local colleges or vocational-technical schools
- State licensing agencies
- Consultants that are "approved" or recommended by endorsement systems

Many other in-service training sources are available, but you need to ensure the hours are fulfilled wisely from high-quality sources. In-service hours are required for a reason—to continually improve and enrich the knowledge and skills of practicing early childhood teachers. Therefore, going to a workshop just because it is all day and will take care of eight hours of your requirement without considering its content, delivery method, and source is a mistake that can have a negative impact on both staff and children. It may take some prodding and pushing, but encouraging staff to spend their in-service hours wisely instead of just looking for the easiest way will pay off in the long run. Not only will the staff and children benefit from the learning and skills development, but also the attitude toward fulfilling in-service hours will become less about "Do we have to?" and more about "When can we?"

Staff Meetings

Staff meetings can be an effective professional development tool that is available to you. Often staff meetings are not organized or planned to their full potential. Many meeting we have led (before we knew better) or observed were peppered with reminders, updates, and other housekeeping tasks, leaving little time for professional development. The highest quality programs we have seen use staff meeting time primarily for networking, problem solving, and professional development. These programs use very little meeting time for administrative items and find other methods to communicate about them.

The key to successful staff meetings is similar to that of professional development for staff as a whole—to consider the way they are valued and perceived. If staff members look forward to meetings as an opportunity for support, team building, and learning (all things that make their jobs easier), then you will be able to facilitate rich and meaningful meetings. But if staff members see meetings as a waste of time (where they will be reminded for the fiftieth time about the proper way to call in when sick), you will not be able to capture their interest or motivate them to learn.

Staff meetings should be planned well in advance. When leading a staff meeting you are wearing yet another hat, that of trainer or facilitator. It takes time and preparation to wear that hat well. When planning the professional development section of the agenda you have many options to consider:

- Should you present?
- Should you bring in a guest speaker? (It's often easier to do so than many think. See page 63.)
- Which staff members should also contribute, and how?
- What materials do you need?
- What outcomes do you hope to see?
- What follow-up will be necessary?

Here is a sample agenda for a staff meeting that focuses on professional development:

September 12—Staff Meeting Agenda

6:00	Meeting Begins/Dinner Is Served
6:00–6:15	Welcome/Announcements
6:15–6:30	Team Building/Icebreaker
6:30–6:45	Problem Solving/Collaborative Work
6:45–7:15	Professional Development Topic
7:15–7:30	Closing/Follow-Up to Ensure Learning

Let's dissect each of the agenda items a bit further.

MEETING BEGINS/DINNER IS SERVED

Starting on time is an indicator of respect to staff *and* a signal to staff of the value you place on the meeting and what will occur during the meeting. In addition to starting on time, as a sign of respect, make sure there are refreshments available. Whether it be a catered dinner, a potluck, or just snacks and drinks, considering and meeting the basic needs of your staff are essential prior to any expectation of learning.

Meeting location is also of key importance. Whether you have the luxury of a dedicated space for staff meetings or use a classroom for the event, consider the needs of adults to help increase their ability to learn. Will they have to squat in child-size chairs? Ask everyone to bring a folding lawn chair or collect them at garage sales or from thrift stores so you have them available. Make sure paper, pencils, or other materials are available. This will help staff learn without disrupting the flow when someone gets up to rummage for a pen. Is the lighting adequate? Does the room smell nice? (Was the garbage taken out before the meeting started?) (Bentham 2008)

WELCOME/ANNOUNCEMENTS

Take time to ease into the meeting, but do so without wasting time. Use the first few minutes to acknowledge any special events or occasions, such as work anniversaries, birthdays, or accomplishments. If you have something to tell everyone at once, for example, that new landscaping mulch is going to be delivered outside Friday or to stop leaving dirty dishes in the sink, you can do that here—although we caution against setting a negative tone at the start of the meeting. Additionally, we propose that you communicate many of these things using other means (see Other Ways to Share the Nitty Gritty, page 64) unless the topic is health or safety related or equally serious or confidential. If your center is experiencing an outbreak of disease or you have news about a particular child or family that all staff members need to know, meeting time is likely the most appropriate time to ensure understanding and confidentiality.

Team Building/Icebreaker

It is helpful to start each meeting with a team-building activity. Before you let out a groan, echoing those of many past center directors and staff, first consider the goal of team building. Team building is about building stronger bonds among your team members, increasing communication, developing trust, improving work relationships, increasing effectiveness, promoting collaboration, and having fun together. Goals we can get behind, right? The groaning comes from the perception that team building equals a silly game. And, to be frank, if it is done just because it's on the agenda instead of being well planned with an intentional goal in mind, it will feel like just a silly game. Here are some things to consider when choosing a team-building activity or icebreaker:

- What is the goal?
- How much time/space/material do we have?
- How do staff members feel about such things as a lot of movement, close contact, or speaking in front of others? (These answers should not prevent you from choosing certain activities, but you may need to take a gradual approach.)
- How competitive are your staff members? (This answer requires you to choose activities appropriately. Aggressive competition can hinder the intended positive affects of team building.)

Here are two examples that further illustrate the idea of purposeful icebreakers.

> **Example 1**

It is the first staff meeting after you've hired three new staff members. Your goals as a leader are to have fun, eliminate natural new-versus-old staff boundaries, and get to know each other. You decide to play Human Bingo—a game where you develop a Bingo board with personal attributes, such as has sung in front of a crowd, can play an instrument, plays a team sport, and so on in each box instead of numbers.

Example 2

You feel that your staff could benefit from working together more collaboratively across classrooms. Your staff tends to form cliques depending on the age group or classroom they work with. Your goals as a leader are to break those barriers and help staff see the value of working with others across age groups and classrooms. You decide to create teams of teachers from different classrooms and ask them to solve a page of riddles.

We hope it is clear that with intention and forethought, team building or ice-breakers can be very purposeful. Of course, it is important to have fun. After all, laughter eases tension and increases learning. Fun in and of itself can be your goal. But fun should not be the only goal every time or staff members will quickly lose interest and the activity's value will be diminished.

A final note about team building and icebreakers—don't ask staff to do anything you wouldn't do. Adult learners must feel safe and respected, as we shared in chapter 3.

PROBLEM SOLVING/COLLABORATIVE WORK

Every early childhood program on the planet encounters a child guidance challenge once in awhile. We say that with the utmost confidence even though we haven't actually collected data. Every program likely has other challenges as well—separation anxiety, special needs, family troubles affecting children, or naptime issues. Perhaps they even have nonchild issues like parents not following a policy, staff scheduling problems, or somebody hoarding all the construction paper in her classroom. Even though you are the leader, you need not always have the answer, and your staff shouldn't feel as if you do. What is important is that they know you will help them get the answer. One way you can do that is by promoting a collaborative problem-solving atmosphere. The key to making this kind of work succeed is creating an atmosphere that makes it acceptable, even expected, that staff will have challenges and that the brainstorming and solutions staff members generate will also be respected, valued, and attempted.

If you have never implemented something like this before at a staff meeting, take it slowly. Once the habit is established, staff will see the value in collaboration and problem solving and will participate more readily. Until then, try the following suggestions to facilitate the process:

- Have an anonymous suggestion box.
- Ask classrooms to present a challenge or problem together.
- Bring up a few issues yourself on behalf of the staff.

Try the following suggestions to solicit participation when brainstorming solutions:

- Ask staff members to write down suggestions individually or in teams and assign a designated person to read them aloud.
- Discourage arguments about whether an idea is good or bad.
- Have "prizes" for staff who offer suggestions or a reward for the staff person who offers the suggestion that is ultimately successful.

The goal is to build an environment that is safe and rewarding so staff will look forward to the opportunity to bring their challenges to the team.

Professional Development Topic

This is the time to introduce new content or to build on prior knowledge. You'll want to consider topic or content areas as well as who will provide the professional development. Carefully observing your classrooms and your teachers on a regular basis will shed light on topics of importance. Additionally, surveying staff and asking them what they would like in terms of training and professional development instead of always deciding for them is a valuable and often well-received approach. If involving staff in planning is new to you, you may find it easier to provide a few options at first rather than leaving the choice wide open, allowing staff to ease into the new collaborative culture. Topics could

- be theoretical, such as what *play-based program* actually means;
- be specific to a content area, such as science activities;
- introduce an idea, such as the project approach;
- focus on child development, such as building self-esteem;
- focus on a teaching skill, such as optimal storytelling or observation and assessment practices; or
- introduce the third-party quality endorsement system process or expectations.

Whatever the focus is, be sure you have determined why it is important for your staff at that time and what you want to achieve at the end of the session.

Who provides the information? Time again, center directors tell us that they feel their staff members learn better from an outside source than from the director. Though there are many viable alternatives, it doesn't mean center directors shouldn't or can't present; it means they should make the best choice for each situation. Consider these options:

- Is there another program director nearby who is dealing with the same issue?
- Could you occasionally swap training services with other directors?
- Have you contacted your local AEYC or resource and referral for suggestions?
- How about parents? For instance, if your topic is science and you have a parent who works for a science-based company, they may be a perfect guest speaker.
- What about the local school district, resource and referral agencies or Early Childhood Family Education (ECFE) organization? Often dollars are allotted to these groups for training and community development.
- Finally, consider your staff members—some may have a wealth of experience to share. An old adage claims you learn best when you teach. As long as you ensure the message will be in line with your program's mission and values, giving staff members the opportunity to teach each other is something to seriously consider, especially after they have just returned from a conference, workshop, or class. This takes care of two objectives at once: providing professional development for the entire staff and helping solidify the new knowledge in the teachers' mind, increasing the chances that they will apply it in their teaching practices and entwine it in their pedagogy.

CLOSING/FOLLOW-UP TO ENSURE LEARNING

A closing is more than cleaning up and saying goodbye. During this time you should answer the question "Now what?" Do you expect to see new science activities in the classroom the next day? Will you be in classrooms to observe whether teacher/child interactions increase self-esteem? What do you want staff members to do with the information? While you can and should trust your teachers as adult learners to make the information meaningful for themselves individually, you should also suggest applications and communicate your expectations. Often this is the portion of the meeting that gets cut if time is running out—and this may very well be one of the most important parts of a meeting. Adults receive messages and information all day long. If they do not immediately understand the purpose and use of the information, the likelihood is high that the information will be lost. With an effective closing and a clear expectation for follow-up, you can prevent that.

Staff meetings are important at all times but they are integral when a program is pursuing third-party quality endorsement. A center culture that embraces staff meetings and expects challenges and development because of them increases your odds of success as you pursue an endorsement.

Other Ways to Share the Nitty Gritty

Some of you may still be asking, "But if I can't talk about the new parking policy at my staff meeting, when can I?" And you should be asking, because in any work environment, employees need details on the policies and practices of their place of employment. It's the grease on the wheel, if you will. Staff memos or newsletters are an ideal vehicle for communicating "black-and-white" information. To ensure compliance, post memos somewhere visible, such as next to the time clock or sign-in sheet, and require everyone to sign off after reading them. Be consistent in how often you post memos. To further increase participation, use acknowledgement time at your staff meetings to recognize the first staff member to follow a new policy or respond to a request in a memo. A well-timed prize, such as a gift certificate or even a homemade coupon, can motivate almost every adult. A candy treat, a $5 gift card for a local restaurant, or a coupon stating, "When redeemed, the director will take out your classroom trash," is all that is needed. These forms of communication should be considered "training"; it's important that you apply adult learning principles as needed and, most importantly, explain why. This practice will be critical when introducing new third-party quality endorsement system criteria so it is important to adopt it beforehand.

Most programs and staff have few problems incorporating in-service and staff meetings into their routines and very often embrace those events. However, when we start discussing formal education, the conversation often becomes contentious. Emotions run high and feelings are tense when teachers are asked or required to increase their level of formal education. These conversations will be less threatening if you cultivate an ongoing culture of learning in your program. Long before your staff members need certain qualifications to meet standards, you will have opened up the dialogue about pursuing additional formal education.

There are a few ways to approach the pursuit of formal education for staff. You could wait until it is required, whether by your board, customer demand, or a third-party quality endorsement system, or you could begin the discussion the moment you hire a new staff person, further enhancing the culture of learning for staff in your program. Formal education is now a critical component of most third-party quality endorsement systems. The longer you wait to focus on formal education among your staff members, the more it will hinder your ability to succeed.

Your success lies very much in how you introduce and perceive the topic. If you say something like "We can't be NAEYC-accredited anymore unless you go back to school!" you'll probably face an uphill climb. On the other hand, you may find it easier if you share research and information about the impact of formal education on teaching practices. For example, the findings in the Impact of Teacher Education on Outcomes in Center-Based Early Childhood Education Program (Kelley and Camilli 2007) show there is often a correlation between teachers' education levels and their practice. Additionally, you should emphasize the professional component. Most professions require ongoing formal education. Before beginning the discussion on formal education, however, be prepared with accurate information about the options available to your staff.

Education Options

A number of options are available for those pursuing formal education in early childhood. The most appropriate option depends on the staff member's current level of education and their goals. This includes you, the center director, as well. Qualifications are important in your role, and your approach to formal education not only helps you personally but also sets a standard for your staff. Directors have an opportunity to achieve further instruction in management and meet the training and accreditation requirements in many states by pursuing a director's credential if they do not have an ECE degree. Research the programs carefully. Two resources with quality director's credential programs are the Minnesota Association for the Education of Young Children (MNAEYC) (www.mnaeyc.org) and NACCP (www.naccp.org). For people new to the role of director, such credentialing can be more valuable than just the credits or training hours it provides, it can provide the director with a wealth of practical information on managing and operating a successful child care program.

For staff members, the first level of education is often a child development associate (CDA), which can be considered equivalent to a technical college certification in child development. Those seeking a CDA must complete coursework and an assessment, including observations by a CDA advisor. For those without any formal education in early childhood or child development, the CDA is a good start, particularly if they're unsure of which degree they will ultimately seek or if they have any hesitation about formal education. A

CDA is a great way to get your feet wet while learning practical skills. Many colleges, technical schools, or local early childhood organizations throughout the country offer a version of the CDA program. Here are two primary characteristics of a CDA to consider when choosing a program:

- Is the CDA program recognized by Council for Professional Recognition? (For further information see www.cdacouncil.org.)
- Are the courses in the CDA program for credit or simply a series of modules? In other words, are they transferable if you want to apply them to another degree program someday? (Many educators don't think of this until it's too late, and then they have to repeat coursework when pursuing an associate's or bachelor's degree.)

Early childhood professionals can also choose to pursue other degree opportunities, such as an associate's, bachelor's, or master's degree in child development or early childhood education. Be sure to obtain your degree from an accredited college or university. Some states have programs offering child development certificates or a CDA equivalent. CDA programs are often available online. But do your research—these programs often do not award credits and are not considered valid when meeting state requirements for a third-party quality endorsement system. See www.teachingstrategies.org or www.naccp.org for some viable online options.

Barriers

Simply knowing the available options doesn't always make the choice to attend college any easier. Working adults face many barriers when pursuing formal education.

TIME

A typical early childhood teacher works forty-plus-hours a week and has a family with children to care for, a home to clean, dinner to cook, bills to pay, pets to care for, and much more. Although many of them would like to pursue formal education, they find it difficult to squeeze in a few hours of class and homework each week. Working with staff to adjust their schedules, if possible, and knowing what options are available—such as online courses or night or weekend classes—will help. Sometimes just having a colleague or friend help plan a schedule to accommodate the demands of school is all that's needed. Time management and delegation options can often be better seen by someone who is not directly involved. Creating a staff "homework haven" can also help. A quiet area at the center with access to resources will allow teachers in school to capitalize on moments they have throughout the day.

MONEY

Finances are a very legitimate barrier to the pursuit of higher education. Fortunately, many options can minimize or eliminate the costs. Many companies have education reimbursement programs. If yours doesn't, consider suggesting one. There may also be some ways to streamline costs. For example, if two or three staff members are pursuing a program at the same time, perhaps textbooks can be shared or traded. Have fun with it and start a collection. One program we know of put an empty jar in the staff lounge and collected loose change to help purchase books for anyone in school. Federal financial aid is also a possibility. Simply having resources handy so teachers can understand their choices may provide the support they need.

FEAR

What if I fail? What if I forgot how to study? What if they tell me I am wrong in what I've been doing for the past five years? Fear is a legitimate barrier to change. It should be recognized, not ignored. If you tell a staff person "Oh, don't worry, you'll do fine," you've done nothing to calm their fears; you've simply sent the message that you don't think they need to talk to you about their fears. Connect them with practice opportunities so they can experience some success and begin to understand their strengths and weaknesses. Remember, some of their fears may be legitimate. They may not possess strong study skills and formal education may be daunting.

UNCERTAINTY ABOUT PERSONAL BENEFIT

What's in it for me? One of the most significant barriers is a lack of understanding or belief that pursuing any type of formal education will benefit the person directly. This barrier should not be underestimated because often, when overcome, other barriers become much less daunting. Uncertainty about personal benefit can be challenging because it is not often clear to people that this is a barrier for them. So let's examine what exactly is in it for them.

When looking to answer "What's in it for me?" some of these responses are quite likely true:

- higher pay
- promotion opportunities

- more career options
- increased confidence
- increased pride
- more respect from peers and superiors
- more credibility
- additional skills to make the job easier
- assurance that teaching methodology will indeed foster positive outcomes for children
- learning new strategies and techniques
- developing ancillary skills and abilities, such as written communication, awareness of own pedagogy, or content area skills in literacy or math, for example

Many teachers tell us that they are too old to go back to school, or they feel that they already know what they need to be successful. Time after time, as teachers with that perspective pursue a higher education, they say things such as, "I never knew I could be so proud of myself," and "This made me a better teacher than I ever thought I could be."

Planning for Professional Development

Beyond just discussing potential gains obtainable through professional development, it may be helpful to write out some goals. You can use the chart created in the in-service section (page 56) to begin.

In-Service and Professional Development Planning Chart, with Goals

	State (or Program) Requirement	Preferred Method	Plan for Achieving	Status	Goal
Julio	40 hours	Attending full-day workshops	May 10, 8 hr. "Creativity in the Classroom"	20 hours as of May 30	**To increase knowledge of ECE art and other content areas**
Renate	40 hours	Child Care Exchange CEU courses	Will review offerings and choose	5 hours as of May 30	**To understand more about typical child development**

	State (or Program) Requirement	Preferred Method	Plan for Achieving	Status	Goal
Jessica	20 hours	Attend evening courses or online resource and referral offerings	Register for 3 evening courses, attend a local AEYC conference	1 course complete by May 30	**To gather more ideas for child guidance**
Mizuki	20 hours	Attend workshops, any time	Contact resource and referral	No hours completed	**To determine whether ECE is a good long-term career**

Writing out goals, whether it be for in-service or formal education, may help make the pursuit of higher education seem like a means to an end, a desirable end that will positively affect the recipient.

Another approach may be to write the goals first and then fill in the other boxes. This technique is most helpful when it is unclear what type of professional development is best for the individual.

In-Service and Professional Development Planning Chart, with Goals

	Goal	State (or Program) Requirement	Preferred Method	Plan for Achieving	Status
Julio	**To increase knowledge of ECE art and other content areas**	40 hours	One class or a workshop	Associate's degree	Contacted community colleges in area
Renate	**To understand more about typical child development**	40 hours	Online	CDA online	Registered

	Goal	State (or Program) Requirement	Preferred Method	Plan for Achieving	Status
Jessica	**To gather more ideas for child guidance**	20 hours	Online	Look into correspondence or online training	Look at Child Care Exchange's Web site, www.childcare exchange.com
Mizuki	**To determine whether ECE is a good long-term career**	20 hours	Group setting	CDA group classes	Contact Council for Professional Recognition, www .cdacouncil.org

Approaching further education in this manner will help adults learn and discover for themselves what is in it for them. This self-discovery and choice always makes learning more meaningful and desirable.

One of the worst ways to motivate someone is to make them feel they have to do something to continue to be valuable. How can a teacher be integral to the program one day and then, because of her qualifications, be less so the next? Well, the answer is she can't, but she can be made to feel that way if administrators aren't careful. If the catalyst to encouraging teachers to change is because "accreditation requires it," many unnecessary and inaccurate feelings may result. Always remember to answer "Why?" Why does accreditation consider qualifications and professional development important? Why should this staff person care?

 PROVE IT SUGGESTIONS

Professional Development

Luckily, many others have successfully maneuvered these barriers and in doing so have led their programs to success with a third-party quality endorsement system. Here are some suggested strategies:

Group Together

Discuss the issue of professional development during the professional development portion of a staff meeting. Ask staff members to reflect on their goals as professionals in early childhood education, the areas they'd like to further develop, and ideas about how they might accomplish that. Introduce the CDA program or associate's degree, depending on the current level of qualifications your staff members have. Encourage a cohort of staff members to enroll and progress through the courses together. They can form study groups, bounce ideas off each other, share books, and more. The workload will be lighter and the celebration livelier when they finish. If an eligible center director can join the cohort, it's even better.

REWARD AND RECOGNITION

If you don't already have one, make sure to establish a reward and recognition program for major accomplishments. As with children, positive reinforcement along each step of the way can help unsure or nervous adults keep going. Enrolling in a program, implementing new ideas in their teaching practices, finishing semesters, getting good grades, and graduating should all be celebrated events.

TRACKING SYSTEM

A companion idea is to keep a visual record of progress and success. Sometimes knowing that everyone will see whether someone really enrolled when they said they would is enough to motivate a person. Although most early childhood education philosophies discourage sticker charts for children, they can often work for adults.

SUPPORT SYSTEM

Be sure that the student has a cheering section and access to resources (whether it's you, books, computers, or all of the above). Additionally, recognize that the student probably had to give something up to fit school into her schedule. Perhaps you could have a job swap board for postings like "Need a babysitter so I can go to class," or "I am going shopping Tuesday. If you need anything give me a list and money by Monday night." Support for one another can be instrumental in many a teacher-student's success.

These are only a few ideas we have seen that make an impact on the attitudes and perceptions toward professional development and its ultimate results. The best ideas will come from your staff. Rather than allow them to ignore or add to the problem, ask them to be part of the solution. The respect and collaboration that evolves will get your program where it needs to be to succeed with a third-party quality endorsement system.

The Role of Professional Development in Third-Party Quality Endorsement

While we hope this information is helpful, you may be asking yourself "What does this have to with pursuing third-party quality endorsement systems?" Here are four primary and critical reasons to focus on professional development:

- The culture you develop by focusing on and valuing professional development will serve you well as you introduce a third-party quality endorsement system. The dedication and effort required to succeed will mirror the dedication and effort put forth toward professional development.
- Professional development requirements or recommendations made by the third-party quality endorsement system will be easier to meet if you have already gotten a head start.
- The staff meeting routine you have established will allow you to introduce and focus on third-party quality endorsement system topics as you proceed through the process.
- The experiences staff have as they pursue third-party quality endorsement are often professional development opportunities in and of themselves. Staff will only be able to recognize and seize these opportunities if you have a well-established environment focused on adult learning and growth.

Sunshine Child Development Center

Good news! Martha and Georgia created large in-service charts and filled them in for each staff member after holding one-on-one discussions with everyone. They will hang the charts in their staff lounge and everyone will celebrate together as staff members complete their goals. Everyone wants to learn and do what is best for children, but the thought of going back to school is daunting. The slow approach to instilling a culture of staff professional development in the program feels like the right approach for this center. Martha is excited about how well the staff members have embraced the idea. Even better, Renate, an assistant teacher, just registered for CDA classes.

Part 2
The Process

After you've determined which third-party quality endorsement system is right for your center and planned an approach toward implementation, you can begin thinking about the tactical aspects of the process. At this point, directors often feel overwhelmed and have many questions: Where do I start? How do I start? Who can help me? What are the right answers? What is the best evidence? How do I find the time for all of this? We attempt to answer these questions and more in the next two chapters, hoping they will serve as a guide, resource, and source of assurance as you proceed. Along with the explanations are checklists, reminders, and tools that will allow you to discover many of the answers on your own.

Keep in mind that this book does not replace the materials and tools provided by the third-party quality endorsement system of your choice. Nevertheless, the advice and guidance here can make the process more manageable.

Overview of the Self-Study Process

Georgia has just downloaded the order form for the NAC self-study binder from the NAC Web site. Martha delegated this task to her yesterday, and Georgia wanted to get it done as soon as possible. Having the NAC binder will help Martha and Georgia keep the accreditation momentum going in their center.

The design of all third-party quality endorsement systems is essentially the same: a set of standards and criteria organized around the various components of early care and education. These can seem a little overwhelming at first and might even give you some cause for concern. At this point you may be asking yourself, how am I ever going to achieve all of this? Often, there are hundreds of criteria, from physical environment to fiscal procedures, and finding a starting point can be tricky. In your role as the initiator and leader of this process, you need to understand what these criteria mean, but also, and most important, understand the purpose and value of the self-study.

No third-party quality endorsement system was intended to be completed in a short time. No matter where your center falls in terms of quality, underestimating the importance of the self-study process will most certainly result in a great struggle to achieve and maintain these standards in the long term. Third-party quality endorsement systems were designed to be studied, savored, and analyzed so the changes you make will be long term and sustainable. The most successful programs have done this.

In this chapter, we will take an in-depth look at the purpose and the value of the self-study and how to find a starting point; make the self-study meaningful so that it has a long-term impact on your program; and evaluate your program against the standards and criteria of the third-party quality endorsement system.

After ordering and receiving your self-study materials, you might find yourself staring at them with some trepidation. Opening the package will mean that you have to get going. Before doing so, read this chapter carefully. We hope that once you have, you will dive into the materials with eager anticipation.

The Purpose of the Self-Study

Let's begin by looking at the purpose of the self-study. In the simplest terms, it gives you and your program time—time to understand the standards and criteria, the involvement of the process, key people, the changes you will make, and the evidence you will collect. For the most part, you have control over the amount of time you take to do this. You get to set the timetable, and that is great news! Be sure to check with your selected third-party quality endorsement system to determine whether the materials have an expiration date to ensure that you complete the self-study within that time span.

In some cases, your timeline might be influenced by the expiration date of a current third-party quality endorsement or by external expectations, such as from state regulations or program owners. Even in these cases, you still control how the expected timeline will unfold. Whatever amount of time you set for yourself (or is set for you), it is yours to control. You won't be the victim of unexpected deadlines and timelines if you recognize this fact. Everything the third-party quality endorsement self-study requires of your program can fit inside this amount of time, whether it is six months or eighteen months. The most successful centers we've worked with all established a final deadline for completing their self-studies. And although it is possible to be somewhat flexible with such a deadline, experience has shown that defining the amount of time your program will use helps maintain the momentum of the self-study. A typical timeline, from ordering the self-study materials to requesting an on-site visit, is twelve months.

The self-study has four main steps:

1. Evaluating current quality levels of your program in comparison to the standards and criteria of the third-party quality endorsement system.
2. Planning improvements needed to fully meet the standards and criteria of the third-party quality endorsement system.
3. Making improvements and changes exactly as you have planned them.

4. Reevaluating quality levels of your program to check whether you've gotten closer to meeting the standards and criteria of the third-party quality endorsement system.

These four steps are circular in nature, in that you will likely repeat them several times during the self-study to meet the standards and criteria. We will discuss these steps in more depth in chapter 6, but for now, let's take a closer look at how to begin the self-study process.

A common mistake many programs make is jumping straight to the third step, making the improvements and changes, without actually knowing what improvements need to be made or how long they're going to take. Typically, such programs start improving their physical environments, spend a lot of money on new stuff, and then consider the self-study complete. These programs often don't achieve their endorsement the first time around. The valuable lessons they learn are that they had no plan, they set and met few goals, and they focused on all the wrong elements. When planning your self-study, take all four steps into account and fully complete all of them within your time frame.

Directors often believe that making the actual physical changes to their program will take up most of the self-study time. In fact, often the opposite is true. To clarify, let's take a deeper look at how to break down the time you have available to accommodate the four major steps in a self-study. As an example, we'll use a nine-month time frame that starts when you receive the materials and ends when you submit the application for your third-party quality endorsement review. Here is a list of possible things to achieve:

- Become familiar with the process, paperwork requirements, and deadlines of the third-party quality endorsement system.
- Read and understand the standards and criteria.
- Compare your current standards with those outlined by the third-party quality endorsement system.
- Identify areas of improvement and formulate appropriate plans to make those improvements.
- Make the actual improvements as you planned them.
- Reevaluate the success of the improvements.

Your nine-month timeline could look something like this:

Month 1

- Read the self-study materials.
- Navigate and understand the tools and resources available in the self-study materials and on the third-party quality endorsement organization's Web site, if applicable.
- Attend any training that might be required by the third-party quality endorsement system.
- Identify standards and criteria you do not fully understand, and get clarification from the third-party organization itself.
- Determine what paperwork is required (and when) by the third-party quality endorsement system.
- Design and develop organizational systems, such as a file box, to collect necessary documentation. (See Document or Evidence Collection in appendix B for an example).
- If desired, locate any training or support groups or available mentors within your community.

Month 2

- Provide introductory information and training to all the key stakeholders in your program who will be involved in or affected by this self-study, including staff, families, board members, or others identified in chapter 2.
- Use the tools and resources in the self-study materials to gather information about how your program measures up compared to the third-party quality endorsement standards and criteria. This may include doing staff and family surveys, classroom inventories, teacher observations, or a review of administrative and financial practices.

Month 3

- Review the information you collected in the surveys, inventories, observations, and reviews in month 2 to identify and list areas of opportunity and improvement.
- Create action plans based on these identified areas. The plans could include training for staff, learning opportunities for parents, to-do lists for specific classrooms, and task lists for program management. The key to successful planning is to include very specific deadlines for the completion of these tasks and lists.

Months 4 to 7

Based on how long the list of areas of opportunity is, your plans for improvement could detail tasks to be completed over a span of three to four months. If tasks are prioritized and deadlines are set, met, and followed up on, completing the action plans should not be an overwhelming or difficult task.

Month 8

- Use the same tools and resources in the self-study materials to reevaluate how close your program has come to the third-party quality endorsement standards and criteria. This step will also highlight any outstanding or new areas of opportunity that need to be addressed.
- Review all action plans to ensure all tasks have been completed.
- Create one final set of action plans made up of any tasks that need to be completed before the third-party quality endorsement review or on-site visit occurs.

Month 9

- Collect all the information you need to complete the application to request an on-site visit or final review from the third-party quality endorsement organization.
- Complete required paperwork and submit it to the third-party quality endorsement organization.

Typically, most third-party quality endorsement organizations will schedule an on-site visit or review with a three- to six-month time frame from when they receive your submission.

Whatever your time frame to complete your self-study, it is a good idea to break it down into bite-size chunks. Before you continue, let's do some time planning.

✔ PROVE IT ACTIVITY #11

Time Planning for the Self-Study

Write the answers on the lines provided.

1. Do you currently have a third-party quality endorsement?_____
   (If no, continue with question 3)

2. If yes, what is the expiration date?_____
   (Many third-party quality endorsement systems require a program to submit paperwork for renewal, like reaccreditation, several months before the actual expiration date to ensure there is sufficient time to schedule a visit and review the results of the visit. This time frame for submitting could be anywhere from three to six months before the expiration date. Please check with your third-party quality endorsement organization to ensure you do not miss any deadlines.)

3. When are you planning to submit your paperwork to request an on-site visit or review? _____

4. How many months do you have to complete your self-study? _____
   (Many third-party quality endorsement organizations prescribe a minimum amount of time for the self-study before submitting for an on-site visit or review. Please check with your third-party quality endorsement organization to make sure you know what this minimum time frame is.)

In appendix B you'll find the Timeline Planner, a form for an eighteen-month timeline. Count out as many months as you have available, then write in the steps you are going to complete during the course of those months. To guide you through this process, review the nine-month time frame example described above.

Planning and writing action plans are important components of the self-study for the director or leader of this process. As described in chapter 3, your role is not about doing the small tasks such as labeling shelves. Your role is larger: to plan, communicate, lead, and follow up. The planning that you have just done to set a timeline will give you a better perspective on pace and direction as you lead your team and your program. A strong vision and forward thinking will help ensure your success in getting everyone on board and meeting the specific dates you have set for your program.

The additional planning you will do later on in the self-study is more detailed and task oriented. This type of planning will ensure the right people are doing the right tasks for the right reasons in a timely manner.

The Value of the Self-Study

When embarking on an improvement process such as a self-study, you need to understand what to do and why each step is essential. Nevertheless, you should also examine the value of the self-study and what benefits it brings to your program, whether or not your program ultimately achieves its third-party quality endorsement. The most important benefit is to the children and, consequently, to their families. This is your ultimate goal.

Specific additional benefits to pursuing, if not achieving, a third-party quality endorsement include

- improving your physical environment
- focusing on health and safety
- putting developmentally appropriate practices in place
- performing a program evaluation
- providing staff training and professional development
- developing opportunities for family and community involvement

Improving Your Physical Environment

The most visible component of a program is its physical environment. This is what families see daily, where teachers work, and where children have their experiences. Classroom environments in particular often reflect not only the practices and beliefs of the teacher but also those of the overall program. Many children spend the majority of their days here, which makes appropriate physical environments especially important. Making improvements to the physical environment is often the first place a program will start during the self-study. However, it may be the area that requires the least amount of work. Using the tools and resources provided by the third-party quality endorsement system will help a program make meaningful changes to the classroom environment. These changes will have a positive impact on the children's learning, as opposed to making changes for the sake of making changes or to beautify the environment. (See chapter 7 for more details.)

Focusing on Health and Safety

Licensing regulations for child care exist in every state, and all include a strong health and safety component. Third-party quality endorsement systems often build on these requirements by adding practices they deem important to their particular endorsement. As a foundation, programs need to meet state regulations for health and safety. They can then expand their practices for the purpose of third-party quality endorsement. In our experience in supporting centers through self-studies, many reported that the incidents of accidents and illnesses significantly decreased as their focus on broader health and safety procedures increased. (See chapter 8 for more details.)

Putting Developmentally Appropriate Practices in Place

A wealth of information is available about developmentally appropriate practices. Some resources are written by the third-party quality endorsement organizations themselves, others by experienced practitioners in the field. The good news is that all third-party quality endorsement standards and criteria are written around these developmentally appropriate practices. By creating training and action plans based on these standards and criteria, your program will be tapping into the latest and most widely accepted research on developmentally appropriate practices. (See chapter 9 for more information.)

Performing a Program Evaluation

The process of evaluating the quality of your program during the self-study can be very illuminating and is often the catalyst for bringing about change within the program. By identifying areas of opportunity, you can plan targeted improvements to the quality of the services you provide. Curriculum implementation, customer service, and teacher skills take an upward turn because steps and procedures put in place make your program better.

Supplementary benefits of evaluating your program may come in the form of teachers and management staff taking responsibility for their own self-improvement. No one likes to feel that she is not doing her best, and this sense of performance will propel changes for the better. For example, a teacher evaluates the health and safety practices in her classroom and finds that some aspects are not as good as they could be. The teacher may begin to implement small changes in her practices without being told to do so. Thus, even if your program were to delay submission and actual achievement of a third-party quality endorsement, the acts of evaluation and self-evaluation will bring about some changes. (See chapter 8 for more details on health and safety. See also chapter 10 for details on assessment of learning and development.)

Providing Staff Training and Professional Development

Many third-party quality endorsement systems include minimum teacher and manager education qualifications. A better qualified teaching and management staff is one of the foundational pieces to providing a higher level of care and education for young children. Through such requirements, third-party quality endorsement systems are redefining what it means to be an early childhood teacher. Using this information, programs can work toward describing the qualification requirements for their staff, as well as provide adequate opportunities for professional development. (See chapters 4 and 10 for more information.)

Developing Opportunities for Family and Community Involvement

Programs are often remiss in not involving families and the larger community in their activities beyond parent-teacher conferences, holiday programs, or visits from the fire department. The standards and criteria in most third-party quality endorsement systems include a section on community involvement and help programs plan meaningful activities to this end. An added benefit is that families become more involved with the program. The participatory nature of surveys alone often increases communication with families who are sometimes unaware of how they can get involved. (See chapter 11 for more details.)

Sunshine Child Development Center

*Martha, Georgia, and the teaching team are dedicated to getting organized and iden-
tifying their resources from the start. They are certain this will make their pursuit of NAC
accreditation easier. Plus, it will allow them to identify what needs to be done and prioritize those tasks effectively. Martha put her delegation skills to use: a few teachers created
a timeline and posted it on the wall in the staff longue so the entire staff can keep track of
the program's progress. Other staff members began organizing a file box for document
collection.*

"After this, all we have left to do is complete the self-study," says Georgia.

"Oh, is that all?" chuckles Martha.

Using the Self-Study Materials

Martha and Georgia are sitting in the staff lounge with the NAC self-study materials in front of them. They've identified the documentation they need to complete and the tasks they need to get done during the self-study and are negotiating the order in which to do them. Martha has one idea and Georgia has another. Both know that they have to get all the stakeholders in their program involved, but getting started can be a bit confusing. Martha notices the additional tabs in the NAC binder titled "Instructions" and "Information," and turns to those.

"Before we go any further, Georgia, let's read these first," she says.

Georgia laughs and agrees, "When in doubt, read the instructions!"

Have you found yourself in this boat? You have the self-study materials. In fact you've read them, yet you're still confused about exactly how to use all the forms, surveys, and evaluations.

In the chapter 5 process overview, we noted the four steps to completing a self-study. These steps ask you to do very specific things to ensure continuity and task completion. You will use the materials provided by the third-party quality endorsement system as instructed, as they are often reviewed during the on-site assessment visit. In this chapter, we discuss these self-study materials in broad terms and provide you with some best practices on how to complete them.

Keeping track of where you are in the process can be a bit daunting when dealing with the daily details of tasks and separate action plans. To maintain an overview of your progress, use the Self-Study Planning and Progress Checklist in appendix B to track your steps. Make a copy of the checklist and display it in a prominent place in your office. That way you will have a visual reminder to keep you on task.

Let's take another look at the four self-study steps in more detail and see where the materials fit in. Each step has a broad purpose and builds on the previous step.

Self-Study Step 1: Evaluating Current Quality Levels

In this first step, you will undertake a comprehensive evaluation of your program using the third-party quality endorsement system's standards and criteria. The purpose of this evaluation is to determine the starting point in your self-study, and the results will be used to create the action plans for your management team and your teaching staff. Using these specific results will ensure that any work you do to improve your program will directly lead you to meeting the standards and requirements of the third-party quality endorsement system. Remember, this step is about *data collection and information gathering*. You are simply collecting data about your program. At this point you will not need to do anything with the information or start any improvement tasks.

✔ EVALUATING TASK #1

Identify Documentation Tools

Open your self-study materials and list the documentation tools provided to conduct your evaluation. Look for items such as staff surveys, parent/family surveys, classroom observations, physical environment checklists, administrative procedures checklists, and so on. List what you find here:

_____

_____

_____

_____

_____

_____

_____

_____

 **EVALUATING TASK #2**

Assign Documentation Tasks

Assign staff to complete each of the documents listed in Task #1 and determine when they should be completed, keeping in mind that many tasks may need to be completed more than once. The first line provides an example of how to use the chart.

Documentation Task List

Name of Document *(Example)*	Who Completes It?	By When?
Staff surveys	*All center staff*	*Next staff meeting (10/1)*
_____	_____	_____
_____	_____	_____
_____	_____	_____
_____	_____	_____
_____	_____	_____
_____	_____	_____
_____	_____	_____
_____	_____	_____
_____	_____	_____
_____	_____	_____
_____	_____	_____

- -

☑ **EVALUATING TASK #3**

Complete the Documentation

Now that you have determined who will do what, the next task will be to complete the documents according to your plans, keeping in mind that many tasks or areas of opportunity may have to be addressed before they can be completed. As each document is completed, store it in a safe place until everything on your document task list (Task #2) has been completed.

Best Practices: Evaluating Current Quality Levels

Here are some ideas to help you collect the data you need using the self-study materials.

- Stick to the due dates you list on your Documentation Task List (Task #2). This will ensure that all the information you collect will reflect what is happening in your program over the same time frame. Spreading out these evaluation tasks over a long period could give you a skewed overview, given that things can change rapidly from month to month.

- If the third-party quality endorsement system you are using requires staff and family surveys, consider an initial survey to establish a baseline rating. It is not as important to meet the endorsement system's minimums for responses as it is to get an accurate read on the current perspectives of these important groups.

- Avoid sending any surveys or evaluations home with families. It is often a challenge to get them all back in a timely manner. Instead, provide a space and time in your lobby or entrance for families to complete the surveys after they have dropped off their children in the morning or before they pick them up at the end of the day.

- Make it clear to staff members that the first round of staff surveys and observations is not a performance evaluation, but rather a way to find out how the program is performing in comparison to the third-party quality endorsement system's standards. Allow the staff complete anonymity.

- Provide your staff with some guidance on how to self-evaluate. Clarify what it means to fully meet a criteria or standard.

- Avoid prompting your staff with the desired responses to the survey or evaluation questions as this will skew the results.

- Allow staff adequate time to complete the tasks they have been assigned, such as classroom evaluations. Rushing through them will lead to incomplete information.

Self-Study Step 2: Planning Improvements

In this step you will take all the information you collected about your program and create realistic and manageable plans to make improvements. These improvements will bridge the gap between the current state of your program and the expectations of third-party quality endorsement system. Planning is undoubtedly one of the most important things you can do to ensure your success. It gives you a direction, time frame, and clear idea of the exact tasks to accomplish for the remainder of the self-study. In general, you need to create the following types of plans:

- An action plan or list of actionable items for each classroom that covers all the tasks to be completed in terms of health and safety, cleanliness and organization, physical environment, equipment and materials, curriculum delivery, and observation and assessment.
- A training plan for the classroom teachers that covers areas of opportunity highlighted by the classroom evaluations or observations and surveys, such as policies and procedures, teacher-child interactions, child guidance, classroom management, successful transitions, and developmentally appropriate practices, among others. In this case, training may not always be a formal face-to-face session; it may simply be sharing a policy or coaching on a procedure.
- A plan to educate parents on your program's policies, procedures, general operations, classroom practices, and family communication and involvement.
- An action plan for center management to complete the administrative tasks required by the third-party quality endorsement system, such as staff and child file audits, document collection for the on-site visit, staff professional development plans, training logs, and so on.

- -

 **PLANNING TASK #1**

Identify Areas of Opportunity

This task will lead you through the process of finding the information you need to create a master action plan and transferring it to the correct action plan for relevant classrooms or staff.

1. The Family Action Plan
   Make several copies of the Family Action Plan form located in appendix B. Locate your completed family or parent surveys or evaluations,

then go through each survey or evaluation. In the first column of the form, list the criteria or standards numbers to which family members did not answer positively. (See the sample below.)

Sample Family Action Plan

Criteria/ Standards	Training Topics	Training Method and Audience	People Responsible	Completion Date
A.1.a—hand washing procedures				
B.2.d—emergency procedures				

Continue filling in the first column until each criterion or standard receiving a negative response is listed to ensure that you create an action to remediate it. When you are finished, wait to complete the other three columns. You will do those in later steps. Put the Family Action Plan aside, and move on to the Staff Training Plan.

2. The Staff Training Plan

   Make several copies of the Staff Training Plan form located in appendix B. Locate your completed staff surveys or evaluations *and* the classroom observations or evaluations. Go through each and look for criteria or standards that relate specifically to the skills and knowledge that staff members need to effectively do their jobs and meet the third-party quality endorsement system standards. Remember that, in this case, training might be in many different formats. In the first column, list the criteria or standards numbers to which the staff did not answer positively. (See the sample below.)

Sample Staff Training Plan

Criteria/ Standards	Action Tasks	People Responsible	Completion Date
C.1.c—conferences are offered annually			
C.1.b—staff are aware of community resources			

Continue filling in the first column until each related criterion or standard receiving a negative response is listed to ensure that you create a training action to remedy every concern, no matter how trivial.

After reviewing the surveys, move on to the classroom observations and list all the criteria or standards that were not met. You may find that some of these criteria or standards are already listed from the surveys. You do not need to repeat those on your list.

When you are finished, wait to complete the other columns. You will do those in later steps. Put the Staff Training Plan aside for a moment, and move on to the Classroom Action Plan.

3. The Classroom Action Plan

Make several copies of the Classroom Action Plan form located in appendix B for each classroom. Locate your completed classroom observations or evaluations and any checklists reviewing the physical environment of the classroom. Go through each observation and list all the criteria or standards numbers to which the staff did not answer positively in the first column. (See the sample below.)

Sample Classroom Action Plan

Criteria/ Standards	Improvement Tasks	People Responsible	Completion Date
G.4.b—defined learning areas			
G.5.d—age-appropriate manipulatives			

Continue filling in the first column until each related criterion or standard receiving a negative response is listed. When you are done reviewing the classroom observations, move on to any other physical environment checklists and list all the criteria or standards that were not met. You may find that some of these criteria or standards are already listed from the surveys. You do not need to repeat those on your list.

Do this for each individual classroom. When you are finished, wait to complete the other three columns. You will do those in later steps. Put the Classroom Action Plan aside to work on the Director's Action Plan.

4. The Director's Action Plan

   Make several copies of the Director's Action Plan form located in appendix B. Your third-party quality endorsement system will have listed criteria that are related to the general operations and administration of your program. These may be in one document, like the NAC Administrator's Report, or interspersed among various surveys and evaluations you have done. Your first step is to locate all of the administrative and operational criteria or standards. Revisit your Documentation Task List (Evaluating Task #2) to determine which documents contain these criteria or standards. Go through each document and list all criteria or standards numbers that relate specifically to administrative, operational, or management aspects in the first column of the form. (See the sample below.)

Sample Director's Action Plan

Criteria/ Standards	Action Tasks	People Responsible	Completion Date
C.3.f—emergency contact information for each child			
J.1.e—record of each staff member's annual training			

Continue filling in the first column until each related criterion or standard is listed. When you are done reviewing each document, put aside the Director's Action Plan for a moment and reflect on what you have just accomplished. Wait complete the other three columns. You will do those in later steps.

By completing this part of Planning Task #1, you have effectively created a list of everything that needs to be addressed to meet the third-party quality endorsement system's criteria and standards. By listing the tasks, you will have a clear idea of how much work needs to be done and how much time will be needed to complete your self-study. At this point you may realize that you need more (or less) time and more (or fewer) resources than you originally expected. This is valuable information to have at your fingertips, as it will affect budgeting and staffing needs in the long run.

 PLANNING TASK #2

Assign Action Plan Items

Put away all the completed initial surveys, evaluations, and checklists. You don't need them anymore.

Go back to the Family Action Plan (Planning Task #1). For each criterion or standard listed, complete the second and third columns with actionable steps and the name the responsible staff person, as in the sample below. Do not put in any completion dates yet. You will do that later on in the process.

Sample Family Action Plan

Criteria/ Standards	Improvement Tasks	People Responsible	Completion Date
A.1.a—hand washing procedures	1. Post hand washing posters at each hand washing sink 2. Write brief informational paragraph in family newsletter describing center's hand washing policy and classroom procedures	1. Chae 2. Martha	
A.1.c—staff trained in first aid and CPR	1. Make a copy of each staff member's FA/CPR card 2. Have each staff member post FA/CPR card on family board 3. Place a list of all FA/CPR-certified staff members on lobby board	1. Martha 2. All teachers 3. Martha	

Now do the same with the Staff Training Plan, the Classroom Action Plan, and the Director's Action Plan. It is important to designate specific tasks to specific staff members and managers to avoid making your own to-do list too long and unmanageable.

Best Practices: Planning Improvements

- Consider these completed plans as your program's master plan. Your job will be to manage the master plan to make sure that all the tasks get done. (More details on how to accomplish this are described in Step 3: Making Improvements.)

- Give yourself plenty of time to complete this investigating and planning phase. Be very specific and clear as you describe the tasks you are going to do.
- Remember that your program must still perform its daily functions of nurturing, teaching, and caring for the children. This will help you realistically determine deadlines and due dates in step 3 so that you do not overload your teachers or yourself with too much to accomplish.
- Delegate wisely. Look at your staff members' talents and skills. Use this as an opportunity for staff development and assign responsibilities accordingly.
- Follow up on assigned tasks. This is the key to your success! If you set the expectation that tasks must be fully completed in the allotted time and if you regularly check in to ensure that staff members have the time, resources, and skills to be successful, you will quickly see evidence of improvement in your program.
- Encourage team work, collaboration, and problem solving. Allow your staff members to make mistakes along the way, but push them to correct their mistakes too. Be open to suggestions and follow through on your promises. This will ensure staff acceptance of the improvement process and that everyone is working toward a common goal.
- Communicate with your team. Don't make them have to guess what you want to accomplish. With clarity comes cooperation!
- If you create any new program documents such as policies or procedures, put careful thought into the long-term impact on your program, not just on getting through the self-study. Incorporate program, licensing, endorsement system, and other relevant information as applicable. See Developing Policies and Procedures in appendix C for tips.
- Do not attempt to do this all by yourself. Achieving a third-party quality endorsement is a collaborative process and should include your staff and your families. Besides, you will never be able to pull this off by yourself—you would simply become too exhausted!

Self-Study Step 3: Making Improvements

Now comes the part where you actually start making improvements and changes exactly as you have planned! You will work from the master action plan you created in the previous steps.

MAKING IMPROVEMENTS TASK #1

Create Weekly Action Plans

In this task you will select items from your master plan and write out weekly action plans for everyone involved. The purpose of breaking it down like this is to ensure that staff members don't get overwhelmed by the scope of the work, that you as the manager have manageable goals to follow up on, and that you have action plans that can realistically be accomplished in one week. Write an action plan each week until all the tasks on your master action plan are done. It is more effective to do these week by week rather than all at once, because doing so will give you the flexibility to redo tasks or add unfinished tasks back into your master action plan. Here's how to get started:

- Make a copy of the Family Action Plan form located in appendix B. Write the dates of the week on the top, for example, September 15–19.
- Refer to your completed Family Action Plan and select a few tasks that you think can be accomplished that week. Write them on the blank Family Action Plan and also fill in the last column to reflect the date on which the task is to be completed.
- On your master action plan, highlight the items you have selected for the week.

Do the same for the Staff Training Plan, individual Classroom Action Plan, and Director's Action Plan. Now you are ready to go!

 MAKING IMPROVEMENTS TASK #2

Complete Weekly Action Plan Tasks

Distribute the weekly action plans. Review the tasks with the appropriate staff members to check for their understanding. As the week progresses, check in with each staff member to see how each is doing with her tasks. Provide support, resources, and motivation as needed throughout the week. At the end of the week, collect the plans to make sure that all tasks are fully completed. Cross off completed tasks on your master plan. Additionally, on Friday, write up the next week's action plan, and distribute these on the following Monday to all staff members. Keep items on the plan that were not fully completed the week before. Continue this weekly process until all the items have been crossed off on your master plan.

Best Practices: Making Improvements

As you can see, your principle responsibility is to manage and maintain your master plan. In doing so, you are providing strategic management to your staff throughout the self-study in areas such as long-term planning and goal-setting. You are also setting expectations of performance, sharing the quality vision, following up on assigned tasks, creating problem-solving opportunities, and setting up an environment for success.

Self-Study Step 4: Reevaluating Quality Levels

Reevaluating the quality levels of your program helps you check how much closer you have come to meeting the standards and criteria of the third-party quality endorsement system.

When you have completed every task listed on your master action plan, you will be ready to reevaluate your center using the same documentation you used in the first step of this process. The purpose of step 4 is to see whether your program now meets the requirements set by the third-party quality endorsement system.

☑ REEVALUATING TASK #1

Revisit the Documentation Task List

Go back to the self-study materials and locate blank copies of all the surveys, evaluations, checklists, and observations required by the third-party quality endorsement system. Refer back to the Documentation Task List you created in Evaluating Task #2. This list will ensure that you use all the documents required by your third-party quality endorsement system.

Documentation Task List

Name of Document	Who Completes It?	By When?
(Example)		
Staff surveys	*All center staff*	*Next staff meeting (10/1)*
_____	_____	_____
_____	_____	_____
_____	_____	_____
_____	_____	_____

_____   _____   _____
_____   _____   _____
_____   _____   _____
_____   _____   _____
_____   _____   _____
_____   _____   _____
_____   _____   _____
_____   _____   _____

- -

✔ REEVALUATING TASK #2

Review the Documentation

When you've finished this second round of surveys, observations, checklists, and evaluations, review the responses to make sure your program meets the standards and criteria of the third-party quality endorsement system. As you read through these documents, list the criteria and standards your program does not yet meet on a blank Family Action Plan, Staff Training Plan, Classroom Action Plan, and Director's Action Plan. These will become your new master plan.

Review the list from Reevaluating Task #1 for the compliance requirements for your third-party quality endorsement system. In many cases, the third-party quality endorsement system states the percentage of family and staff surveys that must be returned and what the percentage of agreement should be for the responses.

- -

Sunshine Child Development Center

The Sunshine Child Development Center has 100 enrolled families, so Martha distributes 100 copies of the NAC Parent Survey. NAC requires that at least 60 percent of the enrolled families complete and return a survey. This means that Martha needs to collect a minimum of 60 completed surveys. NAC also requires that of the 60 percent who returned the Parent Survey, at least three quarters (75 percent) respond positively to the survey questions. So, when Martha reviews the completed Parent Survey, she must confirm that each question on the survey has 45 or more yes responses.

Luckily for Martha, she collects 84 completed Parent Surveys and finds that almost all of the questions have 80 or more yes responses. Martha is very pleased!

Just like Martha, you must make sure that you meet the compliance requirements of your third-party quality endorsement system. Read the self-study instructions to find this information and write it down on the form that follows.

☑ **PROVE IT ACTIVITY #12**

Checking Compliance Requirements

Name of Document   Compliance Requirement

_____   _____

_____   _____

_____   _____

_____   _____

_____   _____

_____   _____

_____   _____

_____   _____

_____   _____

☑ **REEVALUATING TASK #3**

Revisit Your Master Plan

In this final task for reevaluating your program against the third-party quality endorsement system standards and criteria, review the new master plan you created during the reevaluation. If you have a long list of items that still need work, then this round of reevaluation is not your final round. Complete the tasks on the new master plan just as you did before—in weekly increments. When finished, go back to Reevaluating Task #1 and redo all the surveys, observations, checklists, and evaluations. Keep doing this until you have few or no negative responses on your surveys, observations, checklists, and evaluations.

Best Practices: Reevaluating Quality Levels

Making improvements and reevaluating your levels of quality are circular by nature, and you should avoid rushing through these steps just to get finished. Creating long-term change and making improvements that will stand the test of time takes time, patience, and commitment.

Make sure you understand the third-party quality endorsement system's paperwork requirements for compliance before starting the reevaluation step. Use the information from this round of surveys, observations, checklists, and evaluations to ensure you meet the required standards and criteria and be prepared to write new master plans for any unmet standards and criteria.

A well-planned and meaningful self-study will create positive changes and improvements that last well beyond the day of the on-site assessment or review. Maintaining the high levels of quality achieved is an ongoing task, but with the procedures put in place during the self-study, your program's long-term success is certainly assured.

Remember that the document collection and review is performed to ensure there is legitimate, accurate evidence that your program meets the standards. This is about proving that you do all the wonderful things you say you do in your program. Careful reflection and consideration is critical for each standard that requires evidence. The goal isn't to scurry around producing paperwork, but to ensure your program really meets the intent of the standard. You will likely make a few changes to your program, but in the end your program will be stronger and higher quality, infused with new and strengthened practices.

Sunshine Child Development Center

Things are hopping in Martha's office. She has just read the guidelines in this chapter and has a clear idea of how to develop a master plan of action. This will help the teachers know what to do, why they are doing it, and when it needs to be done. Just this morning, Shondra, the toddler teacher, mentioned how excited she is to start making improvements to her classroom. That definitely made Martha smile as Shondra was fairly resistant to change at the start of the self-study!

Part 3
The Content

The next five chapters are dedicated to the content common to most third-party quality endorsement systems. Each chapter begins with an overview of its topic. Keep in mind that each third-party quality endorsement system has different terminology, number of criteria, or particular focus regarding these content areas. The overview describes the topic in a way that ensures all readers are on the same page, literally and figuratively, when discussing the subject matter. It describes how the topic should be viewed and considered when going through a third-party quality endorsement process. This overview will also guide you through the rest of each chapter, assuring that you, the reader, and we, the authors, are all working with the same ideas and assumptions.

The chapters also contain information on what each topic area looks like in the classroom or program environment. Questions we often hear from teachers and administrators going through a third-party quality endorsement process are "But what does that look like?" or "What do they want to see?" While each program should embrace its individuality (we are not endorsing one-size-fits-all), some details must be provided for common criteria, to ensure clarity for readers. Not only will this help you and your staff understand the criteria's intent, but it will also help you better identify what will serve as evidence. The more you understand about each topic and the intentions behind it, the easier it will be to understand how your program meets the criteria.

Each chapter includes activities, ideas, and tools to use as you work to improve and enhance your program and encourage staff to develop improved or adapted practices to align with your third-party quality endorsement system's criteria.

Physical Environment

The Sunshine Child Development Center

Staff members want to begin their assessments in their classrooms. They are eager to evaluate the equipment and supplies. However, Martha knows from reading the standards that how the teachers use their environment is as important as what is in it. Martha is planning a careful inventory of each classroom along with some training on the best ways to optimize the environment.

Definition

A program's physical environment encompasses many things. Of course it involves the classroom, including its layout, furnishings, equipment, and facilities, but it also includes the common spaces and their attributes, such as the staff lounge, outdoor playgrounds, safety features, paint quality, and more. The quality and use of all things related to the physical environment is a critical component of all third-party quality endorsement systems.

> The physical environment sets the stage and creates the context for everything that happens in any setting . . .
> (NAEYC 2005d, 9)

Significance

Too often the environment is an afterthought, not well designed or used to its full potential. It is a collection of items, a hodgepodge of furniture, stuff for children to use during "free time," and a place where teachers spend so much of their time they forget to really look around. Or, in an effort to meet every standard and guideline, our spaces become homogenous and institutional, leaving behind the comfort and warmth so important in a learning environment (Curtis and Carter 2003). Ideally, your environment should be treasured and honored as a space where children learn all day long, make their most important discoveries, and nurture their curiosity and wonder. The experiences available to children during their time in the classroom, including free time, are as rich and meaningful as any others and are significantly impacted by the environment.

The physical environment accomplishes many important tasks for children. The environment teaches children in many ways, just as the teachers do. Albert Einstein once said, "Play is the highest form of research." The choices and variety of experiences available to children, the accessibility and placement of furniture and equipment, the quality of materials, and the teacher's purposeful use of them all send strong messages to children, their families, and staff. The physical environment can communicate whether children are welcome, whether their opinions and interests matter, whether they will be safe, and whether they will be happy and comfortable.

The elements important to the physical environment can be divided into distinct categories such as materials, design, and the outdoors—although overlaps exist because what is true in one area may also be true in others. What's most important when considering the physical environment is how each component affects the children. Never again consider the physical environment as a place that you simply learn in; instead consider it a place that you learn in *and* from. The switch from *in* to *in and from* will ensure that you approach all enhancements and adaptations in ways that will increase the quality of care and experience provided for children.

Evaluation

When considering the physical environment we must examine multiple components as well as understand and value the environment's impact as a whole. So while we will discuss each major component of the physical environment separately, it's important to begin thinking of the sum of all the parts. Lilian Katz (1993) suggests a multiperspective approach to this examination. She recommends that we not only look at the messages the environment sends from the top down, but also from the bottom up—from the child's perspective. Do children feel welcome? Is this a place that reflects who they are and who they can become? Is it interesting, safe yet engaging, a place children want to run into with arms wide open, ready to embrace their day?

To really understand this perspective, it is helpful to actually go into a classroom and sit or lie on the floor. (If you don't want to because it's dirty, this should tell you something.) Then look at the room through the eyes of a child. Keeping in mind the whole-environment perspective and both the top-down and bottom-up perspectives, let's examine each of those categories we mentioned: materials, design, and the outdoors.

Materials

Materials are so varied it is hard to discuss them specifically. What is ideal in an infant classroom in an urban setting is very different from what may be ideal for a preschool classroom in a rural setting. But while the actual items may vary, the intent behind and purpose of materials in classrooms should share some commonalities.

When considering materials you should answer three questions:

- Do the materials in the classroom support age-appropriate development?
- Do the materials support development in all learning domains (cognitive, approaches to learning, emotional, social, and physical)?
- Are some of the materials open-ended, meaning could children discover and create things you've never imagined instead of everything having a predetermined purpose? Are some of the materials representational, items a child finds familiar and meaningful?

Answering all of these questions affirmatively is the goal. Here are other considerations within the context of the questions:

- Are materials safe and easy to keep clean?
- Are they accessible to children?
- Can children manipulate and use materials themselves rather have to depend on help from adults?
- Are materials varied and enriched to meet the needs of the children in the classroom and to build or scaffold learning?
- Is the goal of supporting children as they become capable and competent learners considered when selecting materials?
- Is a system of organization present?
- Do materials reflect diversity—cultural, gender, and ability?
- Do materials engage all of a child's senses?
- Are there ample materials creating variety, sparking new interests, and avoiding unnecessary conflict?

Clearly, this is a completely different way to look at materials if your previous approach has been to shop for what you think looks cute or fun, accept donations without supplementing them, or adopt any other approach that does not consider the varied and robust goal of purposefully choosing materials. Spending a lot of money isn't the only way to achieve all of these goals. A simple roll of tape, some fabric swatches, and paper towel rolls can achieve the same goals in a preschool classroom as expensive catalog materials.

Looking at some samples of relevant criteria will help illustrate how these considerations support the goals of third-party quality endorsement systems.

NAEYC 2.G.01: Infants and toddlers/twos are provided varied opportunities and materials to use their senses to learn about objects in the environment, discover that they can make things happen, and solve simple problems.
(NAEYC 2005c, 24)

ECERS-R 8: Gross Motor/5.2 Equipment stimulates a variety of skills.

ECERS-R 19: Fine Motor/5.1 Many developmentally appropriate fine-motor materials of each type are accessible for a substantial portion of the day.
(Harms, Clifford, and Cryer 2005, 39)

NECPA III-71: Are developmentally appropriate unstructured materials (e.g., blocks, boxes, paint, and playdough) and representational toys (e.g., cars, dolls, animals, dishes) regularly provided?
(National Early Childhood Program Accreditation Commission 1994, 119)

If your approach to materials selection, indoor and out, takes into account each of these factors, meeting criteria will be painless. Each third-party quality endorsement system has criteria describing and defining materials expected to be in classrooms and outdoors. Use the tools developed by each system when considering your materials. However, if you'd like to have a preliminary checklist to get started, see the Physical Environment Quick Check in appendix C.

Design

The design of the classroom includes the layout of the materials, furniture, and fixtures; the ambience created by lighting, sound, and so on; and the decor, including general aesthetics and displays.

Layout

The layout deserves more attention than it often gets. Most programs are not blessed with everything they want. Perhaps the room shape is less than ideal, or there is a lack of storage space. Maybe there is little natural lighting, or the bathrooms are down the hall. Nonetheless, it is our obligation to children to turn these spaces into homes away from home, welcoming and engaging spaces for them to grow and develop. The layout includes all of the permanent fixtures and mobile components, such as shelves and rugs.

Although you sometimes can't do much about permanent fixtures (unless your budget includes funds for demolition), you can influence the mobile components—the room arrangement—quite easily. Doing this can have a surprising impact on children's dispositions, behaviors, and explorations. You probably don't want to alter the room arrangement every Friday, but making changes can ensure an optimal layout for the children and add needed enhancement or variety to the classroom.

Determining an organizational structure for the classroom layout is useful in helping you decide what goes where and why. Typically, we see early childhood classrooms arranged into learning centers or interest areas. Whether formally labeled or not, defining these areas and their primary characteristics and objectives (type of activity and skills developed) will lend focus to the layout and arrangement of the room.

LEARNING CENTERS/INTEREST AREAS

Depending on age group, there can be a variety of learning centers or interest areas in the classroom. There are no set-in-stone, right-or-wrong learning centers or interest areas for each classroom. No one will say, "Hey, you don't have an area labeled *math*. We're shutting you down." There are also no rules about names, although again, some are better than others. For example, *home living* or *home center* are adequate names but dramatic play might allow for exploration beyond the home environment. While there are no steadfast rules, some important areas should be considered for the opportunities and experiences they provide for children.

- Infants: large muscle, fine motor, literacy development, sensory, music (these may be areas of focus rather than defined interest areas in an infant classroom)
- Toddlers: blocks, dramatic play, library, art, manipulatives, sensory, music, motor movement

- Preschool/Prekindergarten: writing, library, math/manipulatives, science, blocks, art, dramatic play, sensory, listening center, music

This list is by no means intended to limit the areas in a classroom. If you have an interest area dedicated to adhesives or nutrition or water or anything else that your children learn from and enjoy, continue to pursue that creativity and experience for children. Also, keep in mind that literacy opportunities and books should be found throughout the classroom in all areas.

Finally, consider what children are actually learning from the materials in each interest area. Knowing the intended learning and skill development for each area helps strengthen the role of the environment as the "third teacher."

Let's look at a few common preschool areas and highlight their objectives and characteristics as an example.

Considerations for Learning Centers/Interest Areas

Learning Center/ Interest Area	Characteristics	Learning Objectives/Skills Practiced	Materials Needed (examples)
Library/ Reading Nook/ Literacy	quiet, carpeted, soft elements, cozy space	phonological awareness, prediction, sequencing, story elements, print concepts, begins to make meaning from print, and so on	books (nonfiction, fiction, and big books), magazines, flannel boards, sentence strips, magnetic letters, pillows, story-making supplies
Blocks/ Construction/ Building	noisy, carpeted area, safe area with ample space	cause and effect, problem solving, balance, size/shape, patterns, spatial awareness, geometry, and so on	wooden blocks of various sizes/shapes, foam blocks, rug, maps, pencils, paper, people figurines, animal figurines, rulers, tape measures
Science	quiet, space for two to three, by windows, on floor, near sinks	prediction, cause and effect, physical properties, observation skills, classification, measurement, compare/contrast, and so on	eye droppers, water, cotton balls, shells of different shapes and sizes, magnifying glasses, pine cones, color paddles, feathers

Understanding these characteristics and objectives is essential for any successful teacher and classroom. A simple chart like this one will ensure that the room arrangement is purposeful in its design and that all parties—teachers, assistants, and administrators—are aware of the essential characteristics and important objectives of each area.

Ambience

Ambience is a critical factor that everyone notices but many can't put their finger on when trying to identify potential issues. When you examine the environment through your senses, the ambience is what you notice. Is all the lighting fluorescent or is there natural lighting as well? How does the room smell? (We know how important this one is!) What sounds do you hear? Is there soft music or are there children laughing? Or do you hear music you have to talk over and loud cries? Do you see soft elements and cozy spaces? Ambience affects our perception and our disposition. It is a critical factor in the physical environment.

Decor

Most teachers like to decorate, and they should. Their classrooms are where they practice their craft. They should be proud of what they create and offer for children every day. However, the classroom is more than a display case. The decor should always be intentional and purposeful. Yes, children may respond with a smile to a poster of a cartoon character, but what are they learning? Yes, the handprint hearts for Valentine's Day are cute, but did the children have a positive learning experience? Neither of the above examples is inherently bad. But if you had to choose in a world of limited resources, an art gallery of children's own creations made from crayon scribbles, glued tissue paper, and found objects would be a more valuable and meaningful use of space.

The classroom should be designed with the children in mind and create a sense of comfort, security, welcome, and belonging. Children belong here; this is a place for children—that is the message the classroom should communicate. Even further, these specific children belong here. Communicating that this classroom is theirs—for any given group being cared for at the time—is an important message. Additionally, the classroom should appeal to the senses. Everyone is affected by aesthetics, smells, sounds, and so on. Be mindful of the way your classroom environment affects your senses. We quickly lose track as we spend more time in an environment. (We all know a stinky diaper loses some of its smell if you are in the room with it for awhile, but when you first walk into a room that holds a stinky diaper—woowee.) Adults and children are affected by their senses; however, children aren't yet able to verbalize their needs. Spending ten hours in a loud room with babies crying, music playing, teachers talking, lights glaring, and colors and shapes all around is a lot to take in every day, all day, and it gets tiring. Being mindful of this is important.

Outdoors

Just because it doesn't have walls doesn't mean the outdoor environment is any less important. And just because there are wide open spaces doesn't mean the only thing children should do outside is run around. That said, running around among natural elements should not be undervalued. Children need unstructured, undefined, uncoiled time each day. However, they also can learn amazing and valuable things with a little support from teachers, for example, that the clang, cling, and chime of musical instruments sounds different outside; building a cityscape made of blocks takes on new challenges when there is dirt, grass, sand, or woodchips to contend with; the subject or reflection of an easel painting might be dramatically different; high heels make a different noise on concrete than they do on linoleum; or that a fence could serve as a loom for brightly colored ribbons. Everything mentioned about the physical environment of indoor classrooms can be generally applied to the outdoor spaces.

The outdoors doesn't need defined learning centers, but purposeful materials selection is important. Granted, the outdoor area provides some of its own aesthetics, but keeping toys organized and the space clean is important, both for the senses and as a message about valuing and understanding the outdoor environment. To ensure your program is using the outdoor space optimally ask yourself these questions:

- Do teachers interact with children on the playground?
- Do teachers plan activities a few times a week for outdoor play?
- Are there materials available to bring outdoors, whether they be on a cart, in a box, or stored outside?
- Do you have family policies in place that enforce licensing guidelines about going outside? For example, do you require that children wear shoes every day, or bring weather-appropriate clothing every day, and so on?

These simple considerations will ensure that the outdoors is a valued learning environment for children.

Facilities

Your program's facilities as a whole are also evaluated in the physical environment criteria. From fire extinguishers to frayed carpeting, the health and safety provisions and maintenance of the entire building are important. As educators, our focus is often on classrooms and the educational components of the program. However, without care and concern for our facilities, what we do in the classrooms ceases to matter. If programs don't meet facilities standards and children don't have adequate access to drinking water, rigorous sanitation practices, or a safe outdoor area checked for dangerous plants, we are not doing what's right for children. Therefore, when reviewing these standards do not overlook their importance.

Teachers and the Environment

Finally, it's important to evaluate just how teachers interact with and use the environment:

- Do they understand its impact?
- Do they purposefully enrich their classroom?
- Do they ensure items are accessible and important approaches to learning like persistence and self-regulation are practiced?
- Do they scaffold children's learning (build on prior knowledge) through available materials?
- Do they encourage development in all learning domains?

As the NAEYC requirements urge, "Thoughtful educators continually design and redesign their environmental spaces in ways that support the development of children" (NAEYC 2005d, 41). All of the elements discussed so far in this section will be positively impacted by teachers who respond affirmatively to the questions posed above. To these teachers a box isn't simply a box, it is a spaceship or mouse's house or a robot head, and a classroom isn't just a classroom, it is a place of magic and wonder, of discovery and growth, a museum and a science lab.

Implementation

Defining content is important, but understanding how to examine and adapt it is equally important. What follows is a collection of activities to do with staff to ensure that physical environment criteria are met. The goal is not just to "pass" accreditation but to permanently change their thinking, perspective, and approach. Some activities can take place at staff meetings, others as you work with teachers or teaching teams independently. By no means do we advise doing all of these activities—choose those that best suit your program's needs.

PROVE IT SUGGESTIONS

Physical Environment

THE WHOLE ROOM

Help staff think through and articulate reasons about furniture and learning center placement.

- Draw the shape of each room on different pieces of large paper (chart paper works well) including permanent fixtures such as bathrooms, carpeting, windows, and doors.
- Cut out small shapes that represent classroom furniture such as rugs, shelves, chairs, tables, easels, loft, kitchen, and so on.
- Give each teaching team time to redesign their classroom, keeping in mind which areas are loud, which are quiet, which need windows, which need to be near sinks, and so on.
- When staff members are finished, ask them to explain their design to ensure there is thought and purpose behind their choices.

CHILDREN'S PERSPECTIVE

Evaluate the classroom from a child's perspective. Consider how children view the room through their eyes. Ensure the classroom is designed to meet the children's needs.

- Ask staff to write out a list of things children see or experience in their classroom each day. Lists should include things like art materials, work displays, cozy spaces, and so on.
- Then ask them to sit on the floor in their classrooms with paper and pen. Have them record what they see without raising their head or eyes.
- Compare the lists.
- Discuss whether what they actually saw compares with what they thought they would see.
- Have them develop action plans based on their findings.

WHAT DO YOU SEE?

- Take two sets of photographs in each classroom: one from a standing position (from an adult's perspective) and one set from a sitting position (a child's perspective).
- Ask staff members to compare and contrast the sets of pictures and develop action plans based on their findings.

THE SENSES

Evaluate physical environments through the senses.

- List each of the senses (taste, touch, hearing, smell, and sight) on a piece of flipchart paper.
- Draw a line down the middle of each chart. Label one column with a plus sign (+) and the other with a minus sign (–).
- Ask staff members to list materials in their classrooms that positively affect the senses (soft music, textured pillows, and so on), and items that negatively affect the senses (bad smells, contact paper with gunk under edges, and so on).
- After creating the lists, brainstorm solutions for items in the minus (–) column.

SENSORY SHOP AROUND

Understand the impact of the physical environment on the senses.

- Hand out pens and index cards.
- Ask staff members to write about their favorite places and use their senses to describe them. (Typically staff members are detailed about what they see, smell, hear, taste, and touch, or how a favorite place affects their senses, for example, "I love the beach because of the feel of the sun on my face and the sound of the waves.")
- Discuss the importance of appealing to the senses.

MESSAGES

Evaluate the messages inadvertently sent through the physical environment.

- Label separate pieces of chart paper with the following: *night club, museum, spa, birthday party.*
- Ask what messages each should environment send (for example, nightclub—fun and energetic, spa—relaxing, soothing). Have teachers

list the items they would expect to see at each place that would help convey its message (nightclub—colors, music, and so on).

■ After teachers have completed each list, put up a new list labeled *classroom.*

■ Ask them the same question: what messages should this environment send? (Answers should be something like children belong here, children are valuable, this feels like home, it's fun here). Have them list items they would expect to see to convey those messages.

■ Finally, ask teachers whether their classrooms send these messages and if not, to develop action plans to change.

Materials Evaluation

Help staff think through the learning opportunities classroom materials provide.

■ Ask teachers to record a list of materials from one learning center in their classroom on the left side of a piece of paper (preferably lined). On the right side, ask them to write down what children can learn from the item, keeping in mind that many items should be open-ended and they may not be able to list all of the potential learning opportunities.

■ After making a list for items in one learning center it is helpful to evaluate the other learning centers in the same way.

Criteria Evaluation

Discuss and dissect criteria as a large group rather than individually.

■ Copy the criteria relevant to physical environment and distribute copies to staff.

■ Assign sections of the criteria (three to four items at a time at most) to small groups of staff.

■ Ask them to generate ideas of how to meet the criteria.

■ After approximately fifteen minutes, regroup and ask the small groups to share their thoughts and ideas, being sure to add or alter comments as necessary.

NAC E11: Materials, activities, and interactions promote positive self-esteem.

• Adults and children listen and respond respectfully to others.
• Children's names are used in positive interactions.

- Materials are accessible to children.
- Materials and activities enable children to experience success most of the time.
- Children's artwork is displayed at children's eye level.

(National Accreditation Commission 2007, 55)

Staff could generate ideas such as to encourage listening skills at group time (for example, limit interrupting), make sure 50 percent or more of artwork hangs at the children's eye level, limit use of nicknames or endearments so names are used more often, move toys off high shelves on to accessible shelves, and so on.

PLAY

Understand the value of play, open-ended objects, and the importance of the child-led learning process.

- Gather a variety of open-ended materials such as found objects, recyclable items, and so on. Things such as pipe cleaners, foam peanuts, plastic bottle caps, checkers, twist ties, plastic lids, and tinfoil are great starting points.
- Divide staff into teams of three or four to play with the items. Allow at least fifteen minutes, giving no instruction except to play.
- At the end of the time ask them to tell the others what they did or created.
- Give the teams a few more minutes to list skills they used in play, like problem solving, creativity, spatial awareness, trial and error, compromise, and so on.
- Compare these lists to the assessments you use in the classroom and/ or the criteria related to learning. Most often you will find that during these fifteen minutes, staff members were able to practice many important early learning skills.

OUTDOOR CHALLENGE

Gather ideas about unique outdoor activities and opportunities.

- Challenge each staff person to use materials from a different learning center outside.
- Ask them to record how children used the materials.
- Share the findings at a staff meeting.

CLASSROOM SWAP

Use the expertise of staff members to see a classroom from a new perspective. Assign teachers from different classrooms to evaluate each others' classrooms.

- Use criteria or a self-created checklist.
- Ask staff to evaluate the classroom with and without children in it.
- Before sharing the results, remind staff to be both constructive and open-minded. (This activity can be used to address many topics or issues.)

PROP BOXES

Create a resource of enhancements to use throughout the year to introduce new learning and discovery opportunities for children.

- In conjunction with your staff, develop a list of learning center enhancements (such as office, beauty salon, pet store). Most of the enhancements lend themselves to dramatic play but other areas such as blocks (space, travel) could be considered. Then select a few ideas to start.
- Assign different ideas to different classrooms and ask those teachers to generate possible additions for the prop box.
- The list of ideas should be shared with you, the administrator, and parents who may like to donate items. This is a great way to involve families and the community as well.

CHECKLISTS

Everybody likes a checklist. Use the third-party quality endorsement system's standards and criteria *and* your program's own requirements to create short and focused checklists that staff can use independently and regularly to ensure attention is paid to the physical environment.

The physical environment is a powerful tool at every teacher's fingertips. Successfully navigating third-party quality endorsement system criteria requires that your teaching staff recognize this and continually strive to create an optimal learning and caring environment for children. You can also use the Criteria Evaluation Form in appendix C as a starting point.

The Sunshine Child Development Center

The staff members at the Sunshine Child Development Center thought the most important thing they would get out of assessing their classrooms would be to generate shopping lists. What they learned instead was how they could use the environment as an additional "teacher" in the classroom. Not only were the classroom assessments enlightening but the activities they engaged in at the staff meeting provided new insights. The impact of things such as changing room arrangements or enhancing learning centers to include new materials relevant to current topics or themes was more important than they imagined. Knowing more about how children learn from materials and the environment also helped them plan and equip their rooms appropriately. Now as they list items on a "wish list" they are more thoughtful.

Health and Safety

The Sunshine Child Development Center

Martha and her team of teachers are ready to tackle the health and safety aspect of the NAC self-study. Martha has given the lead teachers, Julio, Magda, Isabel, Elena, Shondra, and Renate the classroom health and safety standards and indicators to review and has instructed them to compile a list of areas of opportunity for their classrooms. Additionally, Martha has assigned Georgia the task of familiarizing herself with the general health and safety standards in the NAC administrator's report. Martha plans to have Georgia oversee the health and safety aspect of their program's improvement plans. By delegating these tasks, Martha ensures that key people in her program are learning the health and safety standards, and ultimately will be able to teach the others about them.

Definition

Health and safety in an early childhood program is defined as those policies, procedures, and practices concerned with the health and safety of the children, their families, and the center staff, including nutrition and both indoor and outdoor facilities.

NAEYC's rationale for including health as a standard in its accreditation is as follows:

> To benefit from education and maintain quality of life, children need to be as healthy as possible. Health is a state of complete physical, oral, mental, and social well-being and not merely the absence of disease or infirmity (World Health Organization 1948). Children depend on adults (who also are as healthy as possible) to make healthy choices for them and to teach them to make healthy choices for themselves. Although some degree of risk taking is desirable

for learning, a quality program prevents hazardous practices and
environments that are likely to result in adverse consequences for
children, staff, families, or communities.
(NAEYC 2005b, 10)

Significance

Health and safety is often considered the foundation of operating a quality
program, which is why all state licensing regulations focus heavily on it. If
a program can't keep its participants as safe and healthy as possible then all
other program goals are immaterial. In most cases, an obvious overlap exists
between state licensing minimum health and safety requirements and the
health and safety requirements of a third-party quality endorsement system.
The major differences between the two are often in the depth and breadth of
how the requirements are described and practiced within the program. For
example, state licensing might require a program to conduct and log regular playground maintenance and safety checks, while a third-party quality
endorsement system might ask for a detailed annual playground safety audit,
like the NAC Health and Safety Standard B16 (NAC 2007).

It is widely recognized in the early care and education field that high
health and safety standards in a quality program are paramount to a child's
developmental success. An environment that is safe and healthy allows
children to learn, explore, and grow. Health and safety involves more than
preventing colds and mopping the floor at the end of the day. Health and
safety standards give children a sense of security, predictability, and engagement with their world and the adults in it. Children spend many hours in
care outside of the home, and therefore often view their "school" as a home
away from home. With this in mind, children need to be able to trust that the
environment provided for them is as good as, if not better than, what they
have at home.

These environments must protect children from all possible harm,
including abuse, neglect, illness, and environmental dangers. The responsibility for this within your program falls to the adults who care for the children.
Teachers, managers, and other support staff must be well versed in the factors
that contribute to children's health and safety. You and your staff must have a
deep knowledge of the state's licensing standards for health and safety as well
as the expectations of the third-party quality endorsement you are pursuing.

Everyone should be aware of why these standards are included. Knowing
and understanding "why" will allow your staff to see the value of high-quality

health and safety practices, which will help ensure that that these practices are followed and maintained in a meaningful way.

It is a common perception (although not always accurate) that children entering group care are susceptible to all kinds of illnesses (as is anyone spending their days in shared spaces with many people) such as colds, ear infections, sinus infections, rashes, coughs, and lice, among others. If the program doesn't focus on health and safety, this perception will come true. Children who are constantly feeling a little "under the weather" are not able to fully participate in the program. These children are often more clingy, irritable, and generally unhappy in a group environment. The result is that their interactions with other children and your staff does not allow for appropriate cognitive, physical, language, social, or emotional development.

Understandably, sick children are less likely to play with others or with the toys or participate in activities provided in the learning environment. They are less likely to run around outside, play games, climb, ride bikes, or generally involve themselves with other children. They may seem withdrawn, uncooperative, and lethargic and may miss out on the many fun things that children do to enhance and encourage their overall development and well-being. While short-term illnesses don't necessarily affect a child's development in a permanent way, constant sickness can result in an array of learned behaviors that can hinder a child's development of skills needed to be successful and independent—another compelling reason to prioritize health and safety in your program.

Let's take an overall look at the elements of health and safety in your program—including cleanliness, physical environment, health and safe practices, nutrition, and supervision—and why these are important to children's development.

Cleanliness

Early care and education programs, whether they are center based or home based, are very busy places, and keeping up with the cleaning is a constant challenge. Children who are exposed to unclean and disorganized environments are more likely to get sick and stay sick due to exposure to viruses and bacteria that proliferate in such environments. Young children are not consumed with keeping their environments neat and clean and most likely will step over a mess rather than clean it up. This is to be expected. Young children don't necessarily have a broader insight into the value of maintaining a clean and organized environment. However, adults do have this understanding, so the responsibility falls to you and your staff. A messy and dirty classroom poses a host of dangers to everyone in it. Illness and contagion, trips and falls, choking, poison, or serious injury can be the result and can affect not only the children but also their families and your staff.

Even though teachers are not trained or skilled in diagnosing health issues, they certainly can provide a clean environment that minimizes these risks. A consistent and regular cleaning plan—which includes daily, weekly, and monthly tasks—will accomplish this. It is imperative that your program maintains cleanliness, whether by the teachers, support staff, or outside services. Many licensing agencies and third-party quality endorsement systems will describe their expectations in some detail. Organizations such as NAEYC list the cleaning expectations for classrooms and the program as a whole in the Health Standard Book in the self-study kit, and NAC supplies a wealth of health information on its Web site (www.naccp.org). Such descriptions will help you evaluate and fine-tune your program's overall cleaning tasks and routines.

Physical Environment

Each morning when children enter your program, they go to the space that is provided for them. This becomes their world—their physical environment—for their time with you, and it should be the safest place possible. Walls, windows, furniture, equipment, toys, exits, fall zones, bathrooms, and floor coverings all play a part. Teachers must be mindful of any dangers these areas might pose, like tripping or choking hazards, or the possibility of getting splinters or cuts, or ingesting unsafe liquids or solids, among others.

Children constantly interact with their environment throughout the day and quickly learn how to react to it. An unsafe or even dangerous environment will affect how children behave and respond to the cues in it. If children are constantly presented with broken toys, they do not learn how to take care of and respect things. If children do not have appropriate and safe furniture and equipment, they may learn unsafe behaviors such as excessive climbing to cope with what they have. If there are items in the environment that have caused injury or choking in the past, children will learn to be distrustful of what is provided for them. These dangers or risks teach children in subtle ways that their world is not a safe place, and this hinders their development and ability to learn.

Health and Safety Practices

Providing a clean and healthy environment is just the start in a high-quality program. Having practices and procedures that promote and maintain safety and health are the real keys to success. When these are in place, children learn valuable skills that extend outside of your program and become the foundation for health and safety practices for the rest of their lives.

Your program should aim to involve the children in learning how to stay safe and healthy as part of the daily life skills modeled for them by your staff. Practices such as cleaning up the classroom after play, being respectful of toys and furniture, washing hands at appropriate times, good toileting habits, taking responsibility for spills and accidents, responding correctly in emergencies, and treating others with respect and kindness all contribute to children learning to live and function safely in the world. If these skills are not taught and practiced on a daily basis, children are denied the opportunity of becoming capable and independent individuals who can care for themselves and others, not only as children but also perhaps later as adults. Part of your teachers' broader and long-term teaching goals should be to encourage these self-reliance and self-care abilities in children as a feature of helping to raise the next generation of healthy, responsible, and caring adults.

Nutrition

Many children spend more than eight hours a day in care outside of the home and are provided meals away from home several times a day. Sometimes families will supply these meals, and sometimes the care provider prepares the meals. In either case, children must have their nutritional needs met to grow and develop appropriately. Much information is available nowadays on what constitutes a healthy diet for children. A credible online source is the MyPyramid Web site (www.mypyramid.gov) administered by the U.S. Department of Agriculture.

High-quality programs must include good nutrition and should include nutrition education for both families and the children. Prevention is better than a cure in this case; providing children with the tools and information to make better choices for themselves is imperative. Teaching children to read their bodies' cues and to tell the difference between foods that are good and bad for them is a significant positive influence child care providers can have. When caregivers are positive role models for children, with regard to food, children are more likely to make appropriate choices for themselves. This positive modeling also strengthens the children's level of trust toward their caregivers, making them more likely to learn from the adults in their world.

Supervision

Children are explorers and adventurers, and the world is a place of constant discovery and wonder. A child's understanding of danger is far different from that of an adult. Supervision is much more than counting children. It includes keeping them safe and away from harm, knowing where they are at all times, ensuring their needs are taken care of, and supporting their exploration. When children are placed in care outside of the home, families expect that adequate supervision is a foundation of the care provided. All state licensing agencies stipulate maximum child-staff ratios as part of their licensing regulations, and third-party quality endorsement systems not only echo the need for these ratios but also often recommend lower ratios, with one reason being to optimize the supervision efforts within each age group.

Adult supervision in a child's world provides them with a sense of security and safety. It tells children that all is well and that they can trust their environment to be safe to explore and learn from. Even when accidents happen—when children trip, tumble, and fall—having adults present and attentive sends a clear message to children that they will be cared for and assisted. Children grow in confidence and independence when the adults in their world are routinely present to support them, include them, challenge and console them. The world seems less scary when an adult is available to meet a child's needs.

Thus, teachers and caregivers must understand that supervision is more than having knowledge of what their teacher-child ratios are and how many children they have in their care at any given time, but also includes knowing what appropriate supervision actually does for the children in their care. Teachers need to engage children in a way that builds trust and encourages them to participate and venture out into the world. Group care can be hard on some children, and they have to develop skills to handle the pace and scope of their day outside of the home. Their teacher and the quality of the supervision provided by that teacher is their most obvious and important influence.

Evaluation

Now that you have a better understanding of why health and safety are important to the children in your program, let's look at common expectations for health and safety in early care and education programs. These can be considered best practices and will easily mesh with the standards in your third-party quality endorsement system. In addition to the classroom practices for health and safety, other standards deal with managing health and safety practices in your program, including things like overall maintenance of facilities, paperwork requirements, insurance, and emergency and disaster preparedness. The best practice standards are grouped in the following way:

- administrative standards for health and safety
- facilities maintenance
- health and safety training for staff
- health and safety in the classroom (indoors and out)
- medication
- food safety and nutrition

You may find that you don't do these things exactly as they are described here. Nevertheless, evaluate your practices while keeping in mind the objective of why this is a best practice. You may find that you actually achieve the objective in a slightly different way, and that's okay. Remember that these best practices don't replace the actual standards and criteria described in your third-party quality endorsement system but are intended to help you get started. You will still need to use the required documentation to complete the self-study process of your third-party quality endorsement. Many endorsement systems have detailed and specific criteria relating to health and safety. Others may not describe these standards with any great detail, relying instead on the program's adherence to licensing standards as confirmation of compliance with health and safety regulations. In either case, these best practices will help you understand the scope of the expectations for a high-quality program.

Administrative Standards for Health and Safety

In this section we examine the common standards for center directors in promoting health and safety. The following checklist can assist you in understanding best practices and comparing your program to them. You will find many correlations with the third-party quality endorsement system you are using. This checklist is not meant to replace the requirements of the endorsement system but rather to give you an overview of commonly accepted health and safety practices in the early childhood education and care field.

✔️ PROVE IT ACTIVITY #13

Administrative Standards Checklist

SECURITY MEASURES

☐ There is a system in place to restrict facility access to staff, families, and other approved persons.

☐ The program has written details and permissions for all adults authorized to pick up children.

☐ A policy is in place and training is provided to ensure that staff members identify any person picking up a child.

☐ Program staff members routinely check the identity of any person unfamiliar to them wishing to pick up a child.

☐ Program staff members are trained to handle situations where they cannot positively identify a person wishing to pick up a child.

☐ The program has immediate access to community assistance (police, ambulance, and so on) in the event of any emergency.

☐ The program has procedures in place to handle environmental emergencies such as floods, earthquakes, tornadoes, hurricanes, fires, lock downs, and so on.

☐ The program staff members keep written records of a child's attendance and location throughout each day.

☐ Family members are required to sign in and out daily to record their child's attendance.

☐ Outdoor areas are secure.

LICENSING COMPLIANCE

☐ The program is licensed by the appropriate state agency for its size and level of service.

☐ The program is in good standing with its state licensing agency and other applicable regulatory bodies.

☐ All required inspections are current and in compliance.

☐ The program maintains current written records for each child as required by the licensing agency and other regulatory bodies (for example, health department).

☐ The program requires a background check on all employees to be completed before they begin work, as required by its state licensing agency.

☐ The program maintains current records for each employee as required by its licensing agency and other regulatory bodies.

☐ The program maintains state-regulated adult-child ratios and group sizes at all times.

☐ The program has a developmental program in place that reflects its educational philosophy.

☐ The program has clear, written policies in place that describe the following:

- nondiscrimination in all its practices
- child guidance
- employees' training and education
- medication dispensing
- emergency plans and medical emergency procedures
- provision of transportation and driver compliance
- training for prevention of child abuse and neglect

Enrollment Procedures

☐ Written information is available for families that describes the program's health and safety policies and procedures.

☐ Families have the opportunity to visit the program before making an enrollment decision.

☐ The program has the ability to include children with special needs, as required by the Americans with Disabilities Act.

☐ The program requires families to provide written information that includes these details:

- child's full name
- child's full address

- name and identification of the child's primary and secondary care-givers in the home environment
- medical information for the child that is necessary for their safety in the program (for example, allergies, special dietary or physical needs)
- child's immunization record
- child's developmental abilities
- name and contact details of the child's health care provider

EMPLOYMENT PROCESS

☐ The program has a clearly described employment process.

☐ The program has minimum age and education requirements for the employment of staff.

☐ The program interviews all applicants prior to employment.

☐ The program requires that any new employee undergo a background check, as required by state licensing requirements.

☐ The program checks references on each applicant prior to employment.

☐ The program requires a documented health assessment (for example, TB test) of all new employees, as required by state licensing requirements.

☐ The program has a clearly written orientation and training program, which includes health and safety topics, in place for all new employees.

EMERGENCY PROCEDURES

☐ The program has a clearly written emergency and medical plan that is available to both staff and families.

☐ The program describes and practices emergency disaster drills on a regular basis.

☐ The program has written evacuation instructions and plans posted at all exits.

☐ The program has an off-site gathering area in the event of an emergency evacuation.

☐ The program has emergency telephone numbers posted at each telephone.

☐ The program has access to community resources that provide additional assistance in maintaining the children's health and safety (for example, local health department, D.A.R.E program, and so on).

☐ The program has clearly written procedures for handling emergency situations (for example, a dangerous person, severe weather, threats, and so on).

☐ The program has sufficient supplies in emergency kits to weather loss of contact with the outside world for twenty-four hours.

☐ The program has well-stocked first aid kits that are easily accessible in the event of an incident or accident and a plan to ensure they are replenished as needed.

☐ Staff members have current pediatric first aid and CPR training.

☐ The program facility has sufficient fire extinguishers, smoke alarms, and carbon monoxide detectors for its size.

☐ The staff is trained in the use of fire extinguishers and other emergency equipment.

FAMILY COMMUNICATION AND INVOLVEMENT

☐ Upon enrollment, the program collects information from the family about the child's dietary, physical, emotional, and developmental needs.

☐ The family is invited to participate in the program's daily activities in ways that would support the health and well-being of their child.

☐ The program has an open-door policy for families to build a relationship of trust and inclusion.

☐ The family is provided with daily information regarding their child's health and well-being.

☐ The program provides verbal and written reports to families in the event that illnesses or accidents occur.

☐ The program provides families with information and opportunities for training in topics related to the health and well-being of their children.

☐ The program partners with the school district or health department to offer health screenings.

- -

Facilities Maintenance

In this section we examine the common standards for maintaining a safe and healthy facility. The checklist below can assist you in understanding best practices and comparing your program to them. You will find many correlations with the third-party quality endorsement system you are using. This checklist is not meant to replace the requirements of the endorsement system but rather to give you an overview of commonly accepted health and safety practices in the early childhood education and care field.

- -

☑ PROVE IT ACTIVITY #14

Facilities Maintenance Checklist

☐ The program has a written maintenance program and schedule in place that includes daily, weekly, monthly, and annual tasks.

☐ The program includes facilities maintenance in its annual budget.

☐ The program maintains current records regarding the maintenance of its facilities.

☐ The facility is in good repair in the following areas:

- The building is structurally safe.
- All window and doors are secure and can be easily opened and closed.
- There is no chipped or peeling paint on walls, doors, window frames, furniture and equipment, fences, or play structures.
- All fixtures are secure and in good working order.
- Emergency lighting is regularly inspected and in working order at all times.

- Smoke and carbon monoxide detectors are regularly inspected and in good working order at all times.
- Furniture and equipment are appropriately sized for each age group and in good repair.
- Large pieces of furniture and shelves are secured or bolted to walls.
- All surfaces are splinter free.
- Bathrooms are in good repair and working order.
- Floor coverings are regularly maintained and free of defects.
- Kitchen equipment and appliances are clean, regularly maintained, and in good working order.
- Air conditioning and heating equipment is safe, regularly maintained, and in good working order.
- Children's toys are in good condition and free of sharp edges, cracks, splinters, and choking hazards.
- Safe storage is available.

☐ The program maintains a pest control program using safe chemicals.

☐ The program has a regular garbage removal schedule.

☐ Garbage containers within the facility are safe and sanitary and hands free for diapers.

☐ The garbage dumpster is inaccessible to children and has a cover to prevent animals from accessing and spreading the garbage.

☐ The program has accessible running water for drinking, food preparation, hand washing, and cleaning purposes.

☐ Hot water that is available to children is maintained at a safe temperature to prevent burns.

☐ The program regularly has the water tested for safety.

☐ The playground is free of hazards:

- Play structures meet minimum state licensing requirements for safety.
- Fall zones around climbing equipment meet minimum state licensing requirements for safety.
- The playground is checked daily before use to ensure no hazards are present.

☐ All riding equipment is in good repair and working order.

☐ There are no dangerous or toxic plants in the play areas.

☐ Gardens are well maintained, attractive, and safe for children.

☐ Program staff participate in daily checks of the facility and outside areas to identify and correct dangers to children.

☐ Children always have access to drinking water.

Health and Safety Training for Staff

In this section we examine the common standards for staff training in health and safety areas. The checklist below can assist you in understanding best practices and comparing your program to them. You will find many correlations with the third-party quality endorsement system you are using. This checklist is not meant to replace the requirements of the endorsement system but rather to give you an overview of commonly accepted health and safety practices in the early childhood education and care field.

☐ Staff is trained in the following areas:

- pediatric first aid and CPR
- SIDS prevention
- universal/standard precautions
- cleaning expectations and routines
- hand washing procedures
- diaper changing and toileting procedures
- prevention and identification of child abuse and neglect
- emergency procedures
- disaster drills
- medication dispensing procedures
- medical device use as applicable (EpiPen, nebulizer, and so on)
- accident or illness prevention and documentation
- food safety
- nutrition for children
- safe lifting
- use of fire extinguishers
- sun safety and sunscreen application
- environmental risks for children

- safe driving and transportation of children
- attendance taking and supervision
- field trip safety
- ADA (Americans with Disabilities Act) requirements

☐ The program maintains current training records for all employees.

☐ The program requires regular refresher training in these topics:

- pediatric first aid and CPR
- prevention and identification of child abuse and neglect
- universal/standard precautions
- sun safety and sunscreen application
- attendance taking and supervision
- emergency procedures

☐ The program has written information available to employees and families regarding its health and safety training.

Health and Safety in the Classroom

In this section we examine the most common standards for health and safety practices in the classroom. The checklist below can assist you in understanding best practices and comparing your program to them. You will find many correlations with the third-party quality endorsement system you are using. This checklist is not meant to replace the requirements of the endorsement system but rather to give you an overview of commonly accepted health and safety practices in the early childhood education and care field.

✓ PROVE IT ACTIVITY #15

Classroom Health and Safety Checklist

☐ Each classroom maintains a regular and consistent daily, weekly, and monthly cleaning and sanitation schedule.

☐ Required hand washing procedures are practiced by children and staff.

☐ Required diaper changing procedures are practiced by staff.

☐ The classroom environment is clutter free.

- [ ] All cleaning solutions and other chemicals are inaccessible to children and are stored in a locked cabinet.

- [ ] Children have access to running water for hand washing and drinking.

- [ ] Hand washing and drinking faucets are separated.

- [ ] Food preparation and diaper changing surfaces are at least six feet apart or separated by a permanent nonporous divider that prevents cross-contamination.

- [ ] Diapering and toileting areas are separated from play areas by at least three feet.

- [ ] Staff uses food service gloves when handling and serving children's food.

- [ ] The program practices family-style dining.

- [ ] Good nutrition is discussed with children at each meal and at snacktime.

- [ ] Food is not stored in classrooms.

- [ ] Medications (other than emergency medication) are not stored in classrooms.

- [ ] All illness, accidents, and incidents are documented and shared with families.

- [ ] Sick children are separated from other children while waiting for pick up.

- [ ] The staff provides daily visual health and well-being checks for all children upon arrival.

- [ ] Children are provided with a rest time.

- [ ] The program provides clean and sanitary napping cots or mats for children.

- [ ] There is a regular laundry schedule in place for sheets, blankets, pillows, soft toys, and other washable classroom items (whether at the center or at home).

☐ The arrangement of the classroom furniture allows for appropriate supervision of children at all times.

☐ Teachers regularly track and record children's attendance and location throughout the day.

☐ Teachers incorporate practice fire and disaster drills into their teaching plans.

☐ When age appropriate, teachers encourage children to participate in creating safety rules for themselves and others.

☐ Teachers never use physical punishment as a form of discipline.

☐ Teachers use the appropriate techniques and practices to prevent and handle situations where children are hurting themselves or others.

☐ Staff checks daily for safety hazards like hanging cords, frayed carpets, overused outlets, uncovered outlets, broken toys, and so on.

Medication

In this section we examine the most common standards for health and safety practices when dispensing and storing medications. The checklist below can assist you in understanding best practices and comparing your program to them. You will find many correlations with the third-party quality endorsement system you are using. This checklist is not meant to replace the requirements of the endorsement system but rather to give you an overview of commonly accepted health and safety practices in the early childhood education and care field.

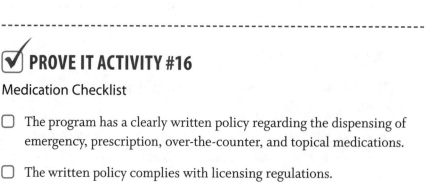

✔ PROVE IT ACTIVITY #16

Medication Checklist

☐ The program has a clearly written policy regarding the dispensing of emergency, prescription, over-the-counter, and topical medications.

☐ The written policy complies with licensing regulations.

☐ The program designates specific staff members to dispense medications.

☐ All staff members are trained in the program's medication policy.

☐ All staff members are trained in the administration of emergency and topical medications.

☐ All staff members are trained in emergency procedures regarding poisoning.

Food Safety and Nutrition

In this section we examine the most common standards for nutrition, nutrition education, and food safety. The checklist below can assist you in understanding best practices and comparing your program to them. You will find many correlations with the third-party quality endorsement system you are using. This checklist is not meant to replace the requirements of the endorsement system but rather to give you an overview of commonly accepted health and safety practices in the early childhood education and care field.

☑ PROVE IT ACTIVITY #17

Food Safety and Nutrition Checklist

☐ The program has a clearly written policy regarding food service and food supplied by families.

☐ When the program provides meals and snacks to the children, a menu is made available for families.

☐ The program maintains current records regarding children's food allergies and dietary needs.

☐ All staff members serving food to children have access to information regarding children's food allergies and dietary needs.

☐ There is a procedure in place for ensuring substitute teachers understand allergies or food restrictions.

Implementation

Making health and safety practices part of the daily functioning of your program is crucial. Odds are many of the best practices are already in your state's minimum licensing standards, so you are probably doing most of these things to some degree already. The next step to making health and safety happen in your program is to compare your state's licensing standards with the health and safety standards and criteria of the third-party quality endorsement system.

 **PROVE IT ACTIVITY #18**

Quality Standards Side-by-Side Comparison

Review your state's licensing standards and regulations regarding health and safety and list them in the left column of the chart below. Then review the third-party quality endorsement system's standards and criteria regarding health and safety and list them in the right column.

Licensing Regulations	Third-Party Quality Endorsement Standards
Administrative standards for health and safety	Administrative standards for health and safety
Facilities maintenance	Facilities maintenance
Health and safety training for staff	Health and safety training for staff
Health and safety in the classroom (indoors and outdoors)	Health and safety in the classroom (indoors and outdoors)

Licensing Regulations	Third-Party Quality Endorsement Standards
Medication	Medication
Food safety and nutrition	Food safety and nutrition

Compare the standards in each category to see which is more stringent, then highlight that standard and draw a line through the other to delete it. If any standards or regulations remain unhighlighted or undeleted on either side, go ahead and highlight those too.

Transcribe the entire list of health and safety standards and regulations onto the Health and Safety Checklist form in appendix C for use in your program. Distribute copies of the completed form to your management team and staff and have them use it for a preliminary audit of their health and safety practices and knowledge.

The Sunshine Child Development Center

Georgia has been working closely with the lead teachers on the health and safety standards in the classrooms. She is excited at the enthusiasm the teachers are displaying. The best part was when Magda and Elena commented that they never realized how broad an area health and safety covers. They used to think it was all about hand washing and staying in ratio. Ah, success! Learning is happening.

Teaching and Learning

Martha is encouraged by the changes and improvements she is seeing in the program. As she implements training on various topics and makes sure staff applies the new ideas to their daily practices, she feels more and more enthusiastic about the process. She thinks staff members feel the same way. Changes to the physical environment and an increased focus on health and safety have already improved the quality of the program and have helped the staff get on board with the process.

That is good news because Martha now plans on evaluating the teaching and learning in each classroom. Teachers are sometimes less receptive to feedback in these areas because it is more personal; it is what they do. They often feel overwhelmed because so many of the standards and indicators are focused on these topics. But Martha also knows evaluation is important and critical to the quality of the program and is dedicated to meeting all of the standards. She plans to start with lots of observations and provide individual feedback to each teacher, helping them grow and develop and ensuring they are providing the best experiences for children.

Definition

Teaching and learning are at the center of what happens in an early childhood program. Quality teaching and learning are the ultimate goals each day. Because of that, they form an all-encompassing topic. Almost everything falls under teaching and learning—certainly the activities we offer, the interactions we have with children as teachers, the delivery and teaching methods we use, the way we develop and offer curriculum, the way we proceed through each day, and so much more.

Teaching is the art of providing experiences and opportunities that encourage skill development and knowledge acquisition. In their early years, when children make new discoveries every day, a primary part of the teacher's role includes making learning meaningful and building children's knowledge. Early childhood teachers are not only responsible for this, but they must understand the varying needs of each child in their classroom and provide experiences that meet the needs of each child.

Learning is a combination of curriculum design and delivery. Curriculum, as mentioned in the definitions section, can be both planned and unplanned.

> The design, content, and implementation of an early childhood curriculum is one of the most significant components of high-quality programming.
> (NAEYC 2005a, 57)

But any old curriculum will not do. While third-party quality endorsement systems do not endorse a particular curriculum, the curriculum used in your program must include certain characteristics to ensure it is developmentally appropriate for the children it is intended for. Applying a constructivist theory emphasizing that children build their own knowledge and understanding of the world based on their experiences, combined with a respect for play as a catalyst for learning, work together as a foundation for curriculum that yields the highest child outcomes. Curriculum is complex; for example, NAEYC's new standards and criteria include eleven topic areas and eighty-eight curriculum-based criteria, and the ECERS has more than one hundred indicators focused on teaching and learning.

Although whole books have been written on these topics, for our purposes it is sufficient to condense them into one chapter emphasizing how they intertwine and impact the children in the program, rather than focus on how they exist separately.

Teaching and Learning Components

We begin by highlighting what components are part of teaching and learning. Because early childhood education has its own language, or brings its own nuances to educational terms, a better understanding of the terminology alone can affect the delivery of teaching and learning in the classroom. These terms bring substance and definition to the goals and practice of teaching and learning in an early childhood classroom.

Curriculum

Curriculum is often considered a predetermined and defined set of learning activities aimed at learning objectives. In early childhood education, curriculum is expanded to include learning and discovery that is child guided as well as teacher guided. It can be spontaneous or intentional. The important factor is that teachers are aware of educational objectives and developmental milestones to ensure the opportunities and experiences children engage in are relevant and developmentally appropriate. Occasional debate surrounds criteria about curriculum with some people arguing that criteria make teaching and learning too scripted in the classroom. Others argue that without some standardization it is impossible to ensure children are meeting early learning standards and important criteria. Whichever side of the argument you fall on, while going through a third-party quality endorsement process be sure that what your children experience in your program does in fact meet the standards and criteria.

Assessment

Although we have dedicated chapter 10 to the topic of assessment, we can't ignore it here. Assessment is an ongoing practice aimed at ensuring that teachers capture the growth and development of children over time and plan accordingly. Assessment goes hand in hand with teaching and learning, so much so that one aspect of a program cannot be optimal without the other.

Teaching Methods

Teaching methods include a multitude of approaches used to transfer knowledge and skill to learners. When a teacher puts materials out on a table and lets children use them in any way they choose, that is a teaching method. When a teacher gathers a small group (rather than a large group or individual children) around the sensory table, that is a teaching method. Whatever means the teacher uses to transfer the information or support practice of skills can be considered a teaching method.

Interactions

The interaction between teachers and children is a significant factor differentiating a low-quality program from a high-quality program. Not only is the nature of an individual interaction important, but so too is the way the teacher guides it. For example, a teacher who sits in the block area with children and asks, "Are you building a tower?" will get a *yes* or *no* answer compared with a teacher who sits in the block area and asks, "Tell me what you are making." The latter will encourage children to think and then articulate their thoughts. These simple interactions are meaningful and will make a big difference in a child's learning.

Learning Domains

The skills and knowledge children practice and achieve can be categorized in different learning domains. In this book we have identified five:

- Social: the way in which children interact and build relationships with others.
- Emotional: the way children manage their feelings, including self-concept and empathy.
- Physical: both small- and large-motor skills, including things like balance and hand-eye coordination.
- Cognitive: mental skills, including language/literacy development, mathematical applications, reasoning, and more.
- Approaches to learning: the way children feel about and approach learning activities. For example, do they persevere? Can they sustain interest? Are they flexible in their approach?

Equal focus on these domains contributes to whole-child development.

Educational Objectives

For each stage of childhood there are objectives, or steps, that are important for children to accomplish before they move to the next stage or step. Each child will practice and master the skills identified in the objectives in their own way and at their own pace.

Developmental Milestones

These are achievements that children accomplish as they grow and develop. They are components of educational objectives. For example, an infant who suddenly crawls reaches a developmental milestone that is part of an educational objective focused on coordinating large muscle movements.

Process/Product

These terms are often applied to children's art but can be applied to all classroom learning and teaching. Process focuses on how you go about doing something and product focuses on what you accomplish. Early childhood education should focus on process in all aspects. The skill development that children gain while experiencing the process and individualizing the process to match their own strengths, needs, and knowledge is more important than everyone getting to the same place.

Developmentally Appropriate Practice (DAP)

As defined by NAEYC, developmentally appropriate practice occurs when programs and teachers provide opportunities based on what is known about child development and learning, what is known about each individual child, and awareness and consideration for the context in which children live. DAP should be the foundation of any high-quality early childhood program (Copple and Bredekamp 2009, 9).

Significance

So why can't children just play? Why can't a clean, fun, healthy, and safe environment be enough? If we could provide that for every child it would be an enormous step in the right direction. When considering the goals of a third-party quality endorsement system, we must remember our intention is to reach the highest quality of care and education. Therefore, research on teaching and learning must be considered. The impact of teachers and curriculum on children's experience, capabilities, self-concept, and growth can't be ignored.

> Early brain and child development research unequivocally demonstrates that human development is powerfully affected by contextual surroundings and experiences. A child's day-to-day experiences affect the structural and functional development of his or her brain, including intelligence and personality. Experiences influence every child's development and learning, and these experiences can be positive or negative, with long-term consequences for the child, family, and society.
> (Committee on Early Childhood, Adoption, and Dependent Care 2005)

Yikes! It's true then—teaching and learning in the classroom do have a significant impact. How adults interact with children is a significant determinant of developmental outcomes.

Teaching

"More than any other variable, instructional interactions define a program's quality and its impact on children's intellectual and social development" (Pianta 1999). And if we didn't believe it before, we must believe it now—teachers and the way they teach make all the difference. A well-equipped classroom, shiny new toys, beautiful playgrounds, and state-of-the-art technology means little without compassionate and competent teachers developing and implementing curriculum in a meaningful way.

But where does play fit in? While we began this section asking, "Why can't children just play?" we didn't at all mean to imply that play isn't valuable. In fact, it's incredibly valuable. As we mentioned in chapter 7, Albert Einstein captured the essence of play in early childhood when he said, "Play is the highest form of research." But play without teachers to support, extend, enhance, and understand it, it is less significant. Consider the following example.

Example

Joshua and Henry are sitting about four feet from one another rolling a beach ball back and forth on the floor. They often do not push it hard enough and it stops midway or they push it too hard and it bounces into one of the boys. They are giggling while they do this and seem to be having a great time.

This is a wonderful and happy experience for these two boys. They are having fun and at the same time acquiring some important scientific knowledge. They are learning how balls move and how to regulate pressure. If a teacher recognizes this, he could do a number of things to enrich this learning experience:

- He could take pictures and show them to the boys a day or two later asking them to recall what they were doing.
- He could offer the boys different balls with varying sizes and weights to roll and ask them to predict how hard they need to push each one.

- He could measure the distance of each roll, marking it with tape on the floor.

And so on. A skilled teacher will know these two children, what they already know, what they have already been exposed to, and what they are capable of understanding. He won't let this valuable moment pass without at least considering his teaching method options. He could also have decided to do nothing, determining that the value of the moment was already being realized in the social interaction and engagement of the boys that allowed them to persist in the activity.

Teaching doesn't always mean intervening. Teaching simply means ensuring that children have the opportunities they need to learn. This might happen during planned group time or in a spontaneous moment of fun between two children playing with fingerpaint.

Implementation

One of the challenges programs face when evaluating their practices is defining and selecting evidence, whether through observation or document collection, to show the teaching and learning that occurs each day. Considering the definitions and research behind teaching and learning, it's important to examine how we put these broader concepts and ideas into practice in the classroom. Let's look at some criteria from different third-party quality endorsement systems to understand fully how to examine and meet them.

NAEYC 2.B.03: Children have varied opportunities to learn the skills needed to regulate their emotions, behavior, and attention.
(NAEYC 2005c, 19)

NECPA III-32: Do teachers focus on individual children and how they have grown developmentally as individuals?
(National Early Childhood Program Accreditation Commission 1994, 110)

NAC F1: Teachers demonstrate behaviors that encourage children's development of trust.
(NAC 2007, 60)

ECERS-R 17-7.1: Staff encourages children to reason throughout the day, using actual events and experience as a basis for concept development.
(Harms, Clifford, and Cryer 2005, 37)

Teachers often know they are providing these opportunities and meeting these criteria but can find it challenging to determine how to "show" that in the classroom. Although no one should do anything just for the visit day, teachers are often stressed when thinking about how they will "prove" to the validator that they meet the standard or criteria. The concepts and ideas that are part of teaching and learning criteria are not as concrete as those found in other categories, such as physical environment. We can't touch reasoning skills. We can't see literacy development. However, we can touch and see evidence that showcases efforts and opportunities aimed at these goals. Helping teachers see how these criteria are practically implemented in everyday situations helps them to accurately evaluate how they meet criteria and to work toward higher levels of compliance and ultimately higher quality in their classrooms.

Let's revisit the criteria listed above and determine relevant evidence.

NAEYC 2.B.03: Children have varied opportunities to learn the skills needed to regulate their emotions, behavior, and attention.
(NAEYC 2005c, 19)

Evidence: Assessors can see evidence of this criteria by watching teachers support children as they make choices, cope with frustration, manage social situations that require sharing or taking turns, and so on. Lesson plans or activities can provide evidence that demonstrates discussions or practice of reasoning.

NECPA III-32: Do teachers focus on individual children and how they have grown developmentally as individuals ?
(National Early Childhood Program Accreditation Commission 1994, 110)

Evidence: Portfolios, ongoing assessment, or daily observation logs, lesson plans, and teachers' one-on-one interactions with children can showcase compliance with this criteria.

NAC F1: Teachers demonstrate behaviors that encourage children's development of trust.
(NAC 2007, 60)

Evidence: Teachers following through and doing what they say, telling children the truth, following a predictable schedule (a validator could match actual occurrences in the classroom to the posted schedule), treating all children fairly and equally, responding to children quickly and compassionately when they are hurt, and being emotionally predictable themselves can provide evidence of this behavior.

ECERS-R 17-7.1: Staff encourage children to reason throughout the day, using actual events and experiences as a basis for concept development.
(Harms, Clifford, and Cryer 2005, 37)

Evidence: ECERS provides an example of supporting this criteria—children learning sequence as they recall the daily routine, perhaps in a group discussion, pictorial cards sequencing activity, or a dictation exercise where the teacher records what the children say prompting them with questions, such as "What happened next?" It can also be evidenced through activities that require choice or discussions, or through books or games like a weather match that connects the right clothes on a doll to the current weather.

It should be evident that staff members do not have to create elaborate evidence to prove they meet criteria. All that is required is high-quality teaching and learning occurring each day. Validators will see clearly that important things are happening in the classroom and record these findings as such. But equally important is an honest evaluation and reflection of teaching and learning practices to ensure that the highest quality programming is occurring.

Feeling that you do a good job and comparing your work to criteria are two different things. Often the thing that prevents a program from succeeding is a staff member's unwillingness to honestly evaluate their practices in teaching and learning more so than in other areas. Being willing to adjust and improve are the most important tools a teacher has in their toolbox. Using a criteria evaluation form is a helpful way to encourage teachers to reflect on criteria and be thoughtful about how they do or could meet it. Let's look at an example.

Sample Criteria Evaluation Form

Criteria Number: **NAC F-3: Teachers are responsive to children.** **(NAC 2007, 61)**	**Category:** **Interactions between staff and children**

Intent of criteria:
(information from self-study materials and staff discussion)
To ensure children's needs are being met. To make sure that if children need something more, less, or different than what is provided, teachers adapt and meet their needs, and that the adults in the program are there for the children.

How we meet the criteria:
(practical application of criteria intent)
We are expected to always respond to children when they are upset or crying, even if they have instigated the issue. We help children problem solve so they can find their own solutions. When children express a need we don't say, "You are okay," or "You're fine," as a solution but we find out what their true need is and help meet it. We all have interactive conversations with children daily.

Observable evidence (if applicable):
Interactions with children, problem-solving strategies

Documented evidence (if applicable):
Documents and lesson plans based on children's requests/interests, problem-solving policy, respect for children in mission statement

Action plan to meet (if applicable):
Director will observe to ensure all teachers are held accountable for this practice.

You'll find a blank version of the Criteria Evaluation Form in appendix C to use in your own self-study. You can use it for all standards and criteria, but we strongly recommend using it for teaching and learning criteria—those that are the least concrete or the most complex and benefit from teacher thought and reflection.

While the standards and criteria in the teaching and learning categories are complex, they can be broken down into smaller parts. When we think about teaching, regardless of the content, we can identify many times when "teaching" occurs in a classroom. Let's focus on teaching methods for a moment.

PROVE IT ACTIVITY #19

Quick Quiz—When Is a Teacher Teaching?

Answer *yes* or *no* to the following questions:

Is a teacher teaching in this situation?	Yes	No
When she is sitting with the children at group time		
When she is chatting with a coworker on the playground		
When she announces how much she doesn't like what is for lunch		
When she calls in sick three days in a row		
When she puts new painting tools out in the art center		
When she asks the children to sing the song she taught them yesterday		
When she puts the "good" books away in the closet for teachers only		
When she enthusiastically welcomes children to class in the morning		
When she responds to a crying infant		

We hope you answered *yes* to all of them. For good or bad, a teacher teaches all the time. This is a huge responsibility, yet one that becomes easier once it is recognized. While teachers are always teaching, we can break their teaching into a few distinct categories for examination.

Relationships

The relationships teachers develop with the children are paramount. Teaching in early childhood cannot be devoid of a personal connection. Whereas a high school English teacher may be able to stand at the board, lead the class from the front of the room, and know only about her student's lives in her classroom (this is not recommended, mind you, but some teachers get away with it), the early childhood teacher would do her students a gross disservice if she tried that approach. In fact, she wouldn't be able to teach. Having a strong trust in and attachment to caregivers is critical in a child's early years. As the NAEYC manual on relationship standards explains, "A solid and positive relationship with nurturing early childhood professionals provides children with a secure base from which to grow and learn, both socially and academically" (NAEYC 2005e, 46). Early childhood professionals who don't understand and value this great gift and responsibility should reassess their commitment to the field.

Teaching Methods

Teachers have many methods of instruction available to them. Whether using simple questions to promote thinking skills, enhancing learning centers to provide opportunity for new vocabulary and experiments, or playing peek-a-boo with an infant, teachers can give each moment meaning if their approach is purposeful and intentional. Teachers should be able to articulate the "why" behind all they do in the classroom; these "whys" are their teaching methods or methodology. We describe a few common early childhood teaching methods below.

SCAFFOLDING

Scaffolding is an important technique that stems from the research of Lev Vygotsky. When a teacher understands what is developmentally appropriate for a child and what that individual child already knows or can do, they provide opportunities to take the next step, to learn the next logical skill. For example, an infant first learns to crawl, then walk, then run. Infants don't go from sitting to running and we don't expect them to. Instead we scaffold this development, encouraging them to build their skills incrementally. Scaffolding is a valuable teaching method, but it can be used successfully only if a teacher understands child development and is attuned to the individual children in her class.

GROUPING

Children learn a lot from their peers. Social interactions and social skills affect all other learning. Teachers can decide how and when children should work as a large group (never for infants), a small group, in pairs, or individually—or allow children to choose. Story time with a large group versus story time with an individual child has very different effect, and teachers should choose wisely. Group time is an event rather than a place, and group experiences and sizes can make a positive impact on many learning opportunities.

Child- versus Teacher-Directed Experiences

It is important to have a balance of teacher- and child-directed experiences in the classroom. In fact, there is a whole spectrum between them. Teachers sometimes lead activities out of habit or solve problems without thinking about the opportunities they are taking away from children. For example, when two children playing in a dramatic play grocery store are arguing over who gets the cart first, they may automatically look to the teacher to solve the problem. But what if the teacher says, "I understand you both would like to have the cart. That is a problem that needs solving. But I think you can solve it yourselves. Please try to come up with a plan and then share it with me. If you need my help I will work on the plan with you." Of course she should keep an eye on the situation to intervene if fists start flying, but in essence she is allowing them to process and plan by themselves, using their social skills and reasoning abilities. Allowing activities to be more child-directed can lead to exciting discoveries and enthusiastic learners.

Additionally, a few simple, open-ended questions during free play may spark connections that may otherwise be missed. For example, if children use scales to balance things in the science area one day and then find themselves in the block area the next day attempting to build a tall tower, the teacher can ask them 'What did we learn when playing with the scales that might help us here?" With some guidance (not interference), she could help the children transfer knowledge gained in science to new materials and situations. Either way, child- or teacher-directed, learning can be enriched, especially when the teacher uses these methods purposefully.

Scheduling

Teachers teach children a lot through a schedule. They provide a consistent and trustworthy environment by following a schedule from day to day. However, the schedule does not need to be rigid. Teachers must be able to adapt to the children's needs. If an artistic masterpiece is in progress, perhaps cleaning up could wait a bit or doesn't even need to happen until the masterpiece is complete and can be shown off. The scheduling of events and time allotted for them is important as well. If children move quickly from one activity to the next, waiting for things to happen, spending hours running around in free play outside, and spending indoor time in teacher-directed activities only, they will not thrive or develop as they could. As the NAEYC manual on teaching standards explains "Creation of a flexible and balanced daily schedule is part of designing an enriched learning environment." (NAEYC 2005f, 56). Though licensing often dictates scheduling nuances, remember that schedules should allow for focused blocks of time and should not be "one size fits all."

TRANSITIONS

Transitions happen every time there is a change in activity, whether for a whole group or an individual child. Transitions are often lost teaching moments—partly because they are underutilized and partly because when they occur abruptly they can undermine the teaching and learning happening before and after the transition.

Consider an active, happy toddler. He is working very hard at the shape sorter, trying to put the square block in the circle hole. That doesn't work so he tries the square block in the . . . Oops! What is happening? He is suddenly whisked away for a diaper change. When he returns to the shape sorter a few minutes later, he is unsure where he left off and so toddles over to dramatic play instead. These types of transitions happen every day, all day. But they don't have to. Teachers have many opportunities to turn transitions into teaching moments. Children can sing, practice recall, or dictate a story while lunch is being passed. Teachers can post learning posters or real-life pictures in bathrooms to discuss during toilet training. A teacher can name body parts while changing an infant's soiled shirt. They can play math games during cleanup, for example, by asking a child "How many red things can you put away?" In the example mentioned earlier, the teacher can point out other shapes in the room during the diaper change and then help the child ease back into their shape sorter activity upon return. These are just some of the ways teachers can capitalize on transition time.

GUIDANCE

An important perspective in education is that child guidance is about teaching and learning and not about punishment. A punished child may not learn the intended lesson. A child who is given the opportunity to learn from mistakes can gain insights and skills that she can apply to future situations. Guidance is repeatedly identified as one of the biggest challenges teachers face. However, appropriate room arrangement, application of developmentally appropriate practices (especially adapting to an individual's needs), and appropriate schedules and transitions eliminate many behavior challenges. Additional remaining challenges should be considered as areas of opportunity or skill development for the child, for example, self-regulation, prosocial skills, flexibility, trust, and so on. The staunch belief and approach that guidance is about teaching eliminates many of these challenges.

This isn't to say that teachers don't face some real guidance challenges. If the challenges extend beyond the program's capabilities, you'll need to work with the family and help them access resources like the school district, early childhood intervention specialists, relevant books, or other specialists with diagnostic knowledge and expertise. Your focus should be on supporting the child to meet the needs they have, allowing them the best opportunities to grow, learn, and develop.

There are many other ways teachers teach, for example, through the environment, as we discussed in chapter 7. The connections are endless, and a great teacher knows that all of his choices affect the children and every connection is important.

Learning

Beyond how they approach teaching, teachers must consider what they are teaching. A wonderful teacher won't succeed if she only sings lullabies and plays peek-a-boo with five-year-olds. Each component of learning is important to consider.

Design and Content

More early childhood curriculums are available than we can count. Some courses are well-known, and some are unique to an individual program. Some are well-planned and structured while others are more fluid. Some prescribe most daily activities and others allow teachers flexibility to plan their day. None of the third-party quality endorsement systems endorse a particular curriculum or prescribe a step-by-step process for developing one. Some are appropriate for young children and some not at all. Whichever curriculum your program is using will be held to the criteria just the same.

Curriculum

The strength of one curriculum over another often lies in its foundation. The curriculum should be designed with a continuum of educational objectives to allow for intentional scaffolding and purposeful development. A program using a curriculum based on emergent philosophy (directed primarily by children's evolving interests) can do this as easily as a program using a purchased curriculum. Whether you are planning ahead or using observation and assessment to look backward, learning in an early childhood classroom should be purposeful and not haphazard.

Additionally, early learning standards can be a great resource. Most states have a document that outlines these standards. Further, knowing what children can and should work on at each stage and how they learn best helps you develop a quality curriculum to ensure the intended delivery is appropriate for the children. Yes, children should begin learning the alphabet, letter recognition, and phonics, but how it should be introduced and how children will best learn it are questions that should shape the curriculum's design. So, whether your program has developed its own curriculum or is using a national program, consider these things to ensure that what you are using is truly of the highest quality.

Evidence of Learning

A classroom should tell a story. The children's work, efforts, progress, accomplishments, and creativity should be evident throughout their space. Learning opportunities can be extended and enriched if children have repeat opportunities to view, reflect on, and take pride in their work. Children who can view their prewriting efforts displayed near them as they sit down at the writing center will be supported by the ability to revisit their previous work. Children whose watercolor easel paintings hang on the wall will take pride in their efforts knowing those efforts were valuable enough to be displayed for all to see. Parents and colleagues should be able to understand what the children are doing based on the evidence displayed in the classroom so they too can support the extension of learning.

School Readiness

School readiness is now a trendy phrase and a sought-after goal in early childhood. It is a worthy goal, since preparing children for success in school is important. However, the intent behind school readiness efforts has been skewed. The focus has become purely academic when it should be on whole-child readiness. The focus has been on kindergarten readiness rather than all of school. It makes sense to think we should be preparing children to succeed at school and in life at all grade levels in all ways. However, the overemphasis on rote learning (letters, numbers, spelling names) is hurting more than helping. Educators must know the true meaning and intent of school readiness and help families to see the stronger value in teaching children life skills such as perseverance, reasoning, and cooperation rather than using flash cards to memorize facts without context.

Here are a few activities you can do with your staff to increase their knowledge and understanding of the impact teaching and learning has and to help them begin to evaluate their own impact.

 **PROVE IT ACTIVITY #20**

Interactions Quiz

Interactions are one of your most important and effective teaching tools. There is a lot to learn about interactions and how to use them effectively in the classroom. This quiz will help you to see where you are and where you need to go.

Interactions Self-Quiz

Statement	Yes, or most of the time	No, or rarely
I sit and talk with children at meal and snacktimes.		
I allow children to make choices.		
I read to children at least two times every day.		
I sing to children.		
I speak to children at their eye level.		
I ask children questions to find out what they are thinking.		
I ask children questions to find out what they are learning.		
I ask children questions to find out about them.		
I verbally welcome all children, parents, and visitors to my classroom.		
I have conversations with children during routine care, such as during hand washing and diapering.		
I choose my words carefully.		
I use positional words (under, before, next to).		
I use children's names more than nicknames.		
I use words to comfort and reassure.		
I use words to help children describe their thoughts, actions, and feelings, and validate them.		
I use interactions to build children's self-confidence.		
My words are positive and not biased.		

Statement	Yes, or most of the time	No, or rarely
I use open-ended questions and comments.		
When I tell children to use their words, I know they know the words they need.		
I limit my use of the word *no*.		
I explain why, even to nonverbal children.		
I use words to solve problems.		
I offer specific praise, such as "I like the choice you made," more often than generic praise, such as "Good job."		

You can find a blank version of the Interactions Self-Quiz in appendix C to survey your staff. Compare results to highlight differences between how they think they teach and how they are perceived. Many times teachers will rate themselves higher than an observer will. Intending to behave one way is important, but actually behaving that way is much more so.

 PROVE IT SUGGESTIONS

Learning

TWENTY QUESTIONS

Play the game Twenty Questions to demonstrate the value of open-ended questions. Think of something obscure but still relevant to you (not related to work). Ask the staff to guess what you are thinking of using yes-or-no questions. If they get to twenty and still can't guess, let them ask any type of question. It sometimes takes a few tries but eventually someone says, "What are you thinking about?" Tell them and explain why. This process demonstrates how much information a person can garner from asking open-ended, rather than closed-ended questions. It also demonstrates how to avoid implications of "doing it wrong" or "failing," as may occur during Twenty Questions or other closed-ended question experiences.

IDEAL LEARNING

Split teachers into five same-sized groups. Give group 1 a picture of a cartoon apple, group 2 a picture of a real apple, group 3 a plastic or home-living apple, group 4 a real apple, and group 5 a real apple with a butter knife. Ask the groups to pretend they have never seen an apple before and to spend one minute recording all they can learn about an apple from the model they have. (Group 5 always learns the most and makes the most accurate observations.) This activity demonstrates how important real-life learning is. End this session by challenging teachers to provide "real apple" experiences to children every day.

Note: It's fun to do this activity with a truly unknown fruit or vegetable, such as star fruit or jicama. Doing so makes the exercise even more realistic and effective since teachers really may be learning about it for the first time.

ACTIVITY PLANNING

Give teachers time to look at next week's or next month's lesson plans or learning objectives, and to think purposefully about how they should teach. Will experiences be teacher or child directed, in a large or small group, and so on? Will they place new materials in a learning center and let children discover them or will they introduce materials at a group time? Whether your program follows an emergent philosophy or structured curriculum, teachers should be thoughtful and purposeful—and therefore intentional—in what, how, and why they do what they do in the classroom.

ACTIVITY REFLECTION

Teachers can learn after an activity has occurred as well. Give teachers time to think about something the children did. Using an activity description form like the one that follows can help teachers reflect and share the important learning that occurred, helping parents as well understand the value and meaning behind play. Spending thoughtful time reflecting will help teachers plan for scaffolding.

Activity or Experience Description

Date:
Activity or experience name:
Materials used:

Activity or Experience Description (cont.)

Purpose of activity or experience:
Outcomes:

It is a good idea to post these descriptions near displays of children's work so family members can also understand the objectives and outcomes.

EVIDENCE OF LEARNING/DOCUMENTATION BOARDS

If teachers are not in the practice of documenting or demonstrating the learning in their classrooms, challenge them to do so. A documentation board should

1. explain what the activity was;
2. explain what the children knew or thought before the activity;
3. show pictures of the activity in progress;
4. display information about what the children know or think after the activity.

Such an exhibit can make the learning come alive for teachers, families, and the children. Having visual evidence also helps children recall the skills they practiced and pick up where they left off instead of starting new.

When in a classroom, always look for evidence of learning—it should be apparent what children are working on and practicing. The evidence makes the classroom meaningful and enriches the entire experience for children.

APPROACHES TO LEARNING

Approaches to learning is a domain that teachers often are less familiar with. List different approaches to learning, such as curiosity, perseverance, sustained interest, and enthusiasm, on separate pieces of chart paper around a room. (Marilou Hyson, in her book *Enthusiastic and Engaged Learners* [2008], offers a more robust list, if you prefer.) Explain each approach and then ask teachers to roam the room and write activity ideas or experiences on each sheet of paper that would promote the development of the topic. Leave the charts in a staff area for a while and ask teachers to pay attention to class-room activities and their relation to approaches to learning. Ask them to add ideas to the lists over time.

These activities are not intended to help teachers develop, design, or deliver better content, but they do give teachers a new understanding of the concepts and intent behind teaching and learning. Teachers who are reflective about their practices and intentional in their actions while balancing skill with content will achieve success for themselves and the children. Think back to when you were in elementary school at a time when personal computers were a novelty. We (the authors) had fifteen-minute turns each week to use the word processor or play Pong. Our teachers didn't have the skills they needed to teach us to succeed on a modern-day computer, but they taught us how to learn, and that skill has served us well.

Sunshine Child Development Center

Martha has completed her classroom observations and is quite interested in the results. She thought she knew everything about each of her classrooms but found that observing classrooms and teachers for long uninterrupted periods provided new insights into each of them. This insight greatly helped as she provided feedback to each teaching team. Martha, Georgia, and the teachers used the results together to plan improvements and enhancements to the classrooms and recognize current successes. Because she was more informed due to the observations and used a collaborative approach, Martha and the staff members all felt very positive about their progress.

Assessment of Learning and Development

> **Sunshine Child Development Center**
>
> *Teachers Julio and Renate have a brilliant idea! After reading the NAC curriculum standards about observation and assessment, they want to redesign the children's portfolios currently used in their classrooms to better meet the NAC requirements. They talk to Martha about this, and she directs them to write a plan for their idea. Julio and Renate spend the next few days developing an outline for the improved way of creating portfolios. Martha indicated that they would use this outline as the foundation for rolling out the plan at this month's staff meeting.*

Definition

Assessment of children's learning in an early childhood program are those policies, procedures, and practices concerned with measuring, documenting, and describing the children's developmental milestones. Gathering information to accomplish successful assessments can be done in many ways, including through teacher observations, anecdotal note taking, sampling children's work, and photographs and video recordings of the children. This information is then compared to widely accepted developmental norms and used to make decisions about the children's further learning needs and educational objectives.

Significance

Child care today is so much more than day care used to be. Research and findings regarding children's brain development and their learning capabilities and needs have driven this field, moving the focus from caretaking to providing developmentally appropriate learning experiences for children. With this in mind, the next logical step is to determine how well children are progressing along the developmental continuum and how well the learning program is meeting their needs.

This is where assessment of children's learning comes in. If your program's goal is to meet the developmental needs of children, then a process should be in place to evaluate whether this is happening. The entire process of assessment must lead your program not only to knowing how each child is developing but to also knowing whether the learning experiences you are providing are appropriate and adequate for each child. The results of this assessment can help you make appropriate decisions about what each child needs in terms of their whole development as well as help you to discover where the learning program must adapt and change to meet those needs. Assessment is not pass/fail or a tool to measure how far children are ahead of or behind schedule. Rather, it is an opportunity to know each child individually and be sure their growth and development is supported.

In regard to assessing children's learning, the 2003 Joint Position Statement of the National Association for the Education of Young Children (NAEYC) and the National Association of Early Childhood Specialists in State Departments of Education (NAECS/SDE) states that those involved in the early childhood profession have the responsibility to "make ethical, appropriate, valid, and reliable assessment a central part of all early childhood programs. To assess young children's strengths, progress, and needs, use assessment methods that are developmentally appropriate, culturally and linguistically responsive, tied to children's daily activities, supported by professional development, inclusive of families, and connected to specific, beneficial purposes: (1) making sound decisions about teaching and learning, (2) identifying significant concerns that may require focused intervention for individual children, and (3) helping programs improve their educational and developmental interventions" (NAEYC and NAECS/SDE 2003, 2).

Third-party quality endorsement systems generally accept that assessment is part of the learning program. Your teachers should be knowledgeable and trained to carry out these assessment functions, and to then interpret and communicate the results based on your program's educational philosophy about how children learn. This is a circular process that is inherently connected to curriculum design and delivery to meet the children's developmental needs.

The Assessment Process

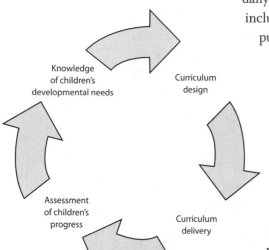

Knowledge of children's developmental needs

Curriculum design

Curriculum delivery

Assessment of children's progress

High-quality early care and education programs incorporate assessment of children's learning into their practices because it completes the circle of strategically meeting the children's individual needs. As a result, the learning program is made meaningful. Best practices in assessing young children's learning include a variety of factors:

- The assessment is not a test of children's knowledge or skills.
- The assessment includes gathering information over time to show evidence of children's progress along a developmental continuum.
- The assessment of children's development occurs in a natural setting of daily activities.
- Teachers deeply understand the program's educational philosophy, educational objectives, and the developmental milestones of children in the physical, cognitive, approaches to learning, social, and emotional domains.
- Families are part of the assessment process.
- The results of assessments are used to make decisions about the types of learning experience included in the learning program.

Evaluation

Your third-party quality endorsement system may have specific standards and criteria that describe the requirements of assessing children's learning. If so, you should become familiar with these and implement them accordingly. However, you can start with some commonly accepted expectations that will move you closer to meeting the third-party quality endorsement standards. These can be considered best practices and will easily mesh with the standards in your quality endorsement. Besides the classroom best practices for assessing children's learning, additional standards deal with managing the assessment practices in your program and include such things as defining and describing your educational philosophy, providing teacher training, keeping records, and involving and communicating with families. The best practice standards are grouped in the following way:

- educational philosophy
- defining the assessment process and plan
- classroom practices
- teacher training
- record keeping and document collection (portfolio)
- involving and communicating with families

You may find that you don't do these things exactly as described here. Nevertheless, evaluate your practices while keeping in mind why this is a best practice. You may find that you achieve the objective in a slightly different way, and that's okay. Remember, these best practices do not replace the actual standards and criteria described in your third-party quality endorsement system—they're only intended to give you a starting point. You will still need to use the required documentation, if necessary, to complete the self-study process. Many of the third-party quality endorsement systems have detailed and specific criteria relating to assessing children's learning, while others may not describe these standards with any great detail. In either case, these best practices will help you understand the scope of the expectations for a high-quality program.

- -

 **PROVE IT ACTIVITY #21**

Assessment of Learning and Development Checklist

EDUCATIONAL PHILOSOPHY

☐ The program clearly defines its belief about how children learn.

☐ The educational philosophy is the basis for the design of the learning program.

☐ The educational philosophy includes all areas of a child's development: physical, cognitive, social, emotional, and approaches to learning.

☐ The educational philosophy is shared with families.

☐ The educational philosophy is an integral part of teacher training.

DEFINING THE ASSESSMENT PROCESS AND PLAN

☐ The program has a clearly written plan that describes the assessment process.

☐ The program has an assessment tool that is used to record the children's progress.

☐ The assessment tool is based on the educational objectives of children at various stages in their development.

☐ The assessment process includes both informal and formal components.

Classroom Practices

☐ The assessment process includes a step in which teachers observe children in a natural setting.

☐ Teachers make and keep ongoing anecdotal notes of their observations.

☐ Teachers collect a variety of evidence of children's progress over time.

☐ Teachers regularly communicate with families regarding their children's progress and developmental needs.

☐ Teachers interpret and use the results of their observations and progress evaluations to individualize learning to meet each child's specific learning needs.

☐ Teachers interpret and use the results of their observations and progress evaluations to make adjustments to the learning program to meet each child's specific learning needs.

☐ Teachers interpret and use the results of their observations and collected evidence of children's learning to complete the formal assessment tool.

Teacher Training

☐ Teachers are provided with initial and ongoing training regarding the following:

- observation and note-taking techniques
- collecting meaningful evidence of children's developmental progress
- using the program's formal written assessment tools
- communicating assessment results with families
- individualizing learning based on assessment results

Record Keeping

☐ The program maintains documentation of children's ongoing assessments.

☐ The program maintains documentation of ongoing communication with families regarding assessment results and the children's developmental needs.

☐ If a program consults with outside assessment professionals, documentation of the evaluations and assessments is maintained in the children's files.

☐ If a program recommends the services of outside assessment professionals to families, the program will ensure that the families' written permission is given and documented beforehand.

☐ The program has a system of collecting evidence, such as a portfolio system, to support a child's growth and development.

INVOLVING AND COMMUNICATING WITH FAMILIES

☐ Family members have regular opportunities to provide information regarding their child's needs and progress.

☐ Teachers and family members have regular opportunities to discuss the assessments of their child's progress.

☐ Family members are given a written record of their child's progress on a regular basis.

☐ The assessment process and conference is not focused on pass/fail but rather on individual development.

☐ Teachers and family members work cooperatively to plan for their child's next learning experiences based on the results of the developmental assessments.

Implementation

Knowing how children are doing as a result of participating in a program or set of services is of critical importance to teachers, parents, program leaders and local, state and federal agencies having responsibilities for the programs. Each of these stakeholders may

have different reasons for needing the information good child assessment can bring, but in the end, the most important stakeholder is the child. The child assessment processes must ultimately bring benefit to the child.
(Council of Chief State School Officers n.d., 4)

For the assessment process to be meaningful and successful in your classrooms, you need to carefully evaluate your current practices against best practices and/or the standards of the third-party quality endorsement you are pursuing. From the results, you will know the areas in which you are already successful and the areas in which opportunities lie. Knowing this is crucial because it will inform your next steps in training your teachers and implementing a comprehensive assessment process, which will have the greatest positive impact on the children. As with each step in the self-study, careful and detailed planning will help you reach your goals in a successful and timely manner.

 PROVE IT ACTIVITY #22

Evaluating Your Assessment of Learning and Development

Begin by evaluating your program's current practices. You can do this in one of two ways:

- use the Assessment of Learning and Development Checklist (Activity #21, page 160), or
- use the standards and criteria for assessing children's learning in your third-party quality endorsement system

Make copies of the checklist or standards and criteria for each classroom and ask teachers to evaluate themselves. Collect these individual evaluations, and then use those copies to conduct your own evaluation of what you observe and know your teachers are doing regarding assessment. After you have gathered this information, you will need to analyze it and use the results to plan your next steps.

1. Complete the following statements to define and describe in writing your desired assessment process based on the requirements of the best practices checklist or the standards and criteria of the third-party quality endorsement system.

Our educational philosophy is

_____

_____

_____

_____

_____

The educational goals of our program are

_____

_____

_____

_____

_____

To support this, our assessment process will have the following elements and considerations:

_____

_____

_____

_____

_____

The assessment standards and criteria required by my third-party quality endorsement system are

_____

_____

_____

_____

_____

2. Summarize the findings of the teachers' and your evaluations of your current assessment of children's learning practices, listing separately the areas of success and the areas of opportunity.

Areas of Success	Areas of Opportunity

3. Using the findings listed in the Areas of Opportunity column, create an action plan to implement new or improved practices around the assessment of children's learning.

Areas of Opportunity	Improvement Activities	People Responsible	Completion Date

Areas of Opportunity	Improvement Activities	People Responsible	Completion Date

4. Put your plan into action. Decide which action items require some teacher training before implementing the change. Be prepared with all the materials and resources your teachers will need before assigning tasks and deadlines. As with all areas of opportunity, add relevant tasks to your master plan and be sure to give your teachers written action plans with clear and reasonable deadlines.

5. Follow up and monitor progress. Provide your teachers with regular and meaningful feedback as they make the changes in their classrooms. Be firm about the deadlines—expect your teachers to complete the tasks set for them by the established date. This will maintain the momentum of the change and ensure that your teachers achieve tangible success.

Collecting Evidence to Show Development Over Time

Regardless of the system of observation and assessment you decide to use in your program, remember that the evidence collected needs to show how growth and development have occurred over a period of time. Recording the results of some observations and whatever the teacher may remember about a child's learning successes and opportunities on a "report card" once a year is an inadequate way of showing meaningful evidence of learning. Most third-party quality endorsement systems will require tangible evidence of growth and development over time; many require portfolios for individual children or for classrooms.

The Portfolio System

A portfolio system is a familiar and relevant method for collecting observations and assessing children's learning and development over time. The term *portfolio* can sometimes be confusing. Staff members often think it is more formal than it needs to be. It is simply documentation and evidence collection. Beyond meeting the requirements of the third-party quality endorsement systems, it is also a tool that informs teachers and families of the developmental progress each child has made over a specific period of time.

Teachers and families can then use this information and evidence to shape the continued and future learning and other developmental interventions for each child. In the early childhood education field, it is a developmentally appropriate practice to *individualize learning* to meet each child's developmental needs. Having a child's portfolio on hand to assist with this is invaluable to the teacher. See NAC standards E4, E5, and E6 (2007), CITA criteria 3.1 and 3.2 (2008), AMS accreditation criteria 4.2 and 4.4 (2008), and others that refer to the use of learner assessment to individualize learning to meet the children's developmental needs.

The portfolio system requires teachers to evaluate the quality of the evidence they are collecting and describe how that evidence shows developmental milestones. Many children's portfolios are crammed full of artwork, writing samples, and other bits and pieces, but the collection as a whole does not show the child's growth or progress in a sequential or meaningful way within the developmental domains. To make the portfolio system worthwhile, consider these points:

- Does your program have a clearly defined system of collecting evidence of children's learning over time?
- Does this system satisfy the requirements of the third-party quality endorsement that you are pursuing? (Even if they don't require child portfolios they often require evaluation of learning over time.)
- Do your teachers know what to look for when collecting evidence of children's growth?
- Does the evidence relate to the learning objectives of your curriculum?

- What do the teachers do with the portfolios when they are considered complete?

Not having definitive answers to all of these questions may suggest that this is an area of opportunity within your program. Validators may review these portfolios and often chat with the teachers about them during their visit. Teachers must understand the concept of showing development over time, not just for the purpose of the validator's on-site visit, because it is a solid teaching practice that is instrumental and crucial in ensuring the children's developmental success.

You can approach the creation of portfolios for children and classrooms in many ways. A child's portfolio can be created as soon as the child enrolls and follow them from classroom to classroom until they graduate. The portfolio can be in a file folder, binder, or something similar. Some endorsement systems also require classroom portfolios. Refer back to your self-study materials and look for specific guidance regarding creation and organization of the portfolios. In some cases such as NAEYC's classroom portfolios, evidence is collected and organized around specific criteria. Guidance documents available on NAEYC's Web site (www.naeyc.org/selfstudy) can help you with this. In other cases, you may find there is no specific guidance available from the third-party quality endorsement system's self-study materials. In that case, portfolios are left to your interpretation. Many comprehensive and useful books are available on this topic and on observation and assessment in general.

Sunshine Child Development Center

What started out as a small plan to redesign the children's portfolios turned into a big interesting project for Julio and Renate. The more they read about the subject, the more they realized how inadequate their current system is. So, instead of just redoing the portfolios, they created a staff training to help everyone better understand how portfolios fit into the cycle of observation and assessment and that they are not just a place to put the children's artwork. They will present their training at this month's staff meeting. Renate is feeling a little nervous about teaching her peers something new, but Julio is convinced they will be as excited as he and Renate are when they learn about this!

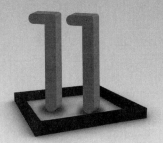

Family and Community Involvement

> ### Sunshine Child Development Center
>
> *Everyone at Sunshine Child Development Center is working hard to make the enhancements and improvements to their program that will allow them to achieve accreditation. Martha and Georgia are busy gathering documents and planning support and training opportunities for staff. The teachers are evaluating their classrooms and altering their daily teaching practices and classroom environments to ensure alignment with accreditation standards. It is a busy time and everyone feels proud of their progress so far—until one day when a parent stops Martha in the hallway and says, "In a previous newsletter, you mentioned that the center was pursuing accreditation. Has that started yet? Is anything happening?" Martha realizes that as busy as they have been at the Sunshine Child Development Center, they have neglected a critical component of the process—to fully involve the families beyond having them complete the parent surveys. Martha knows it is important to involve families in the accreditation process and to ensure their program's family communication and partnership opportunities are the best they can be every day. She put the issue on her next staff meeting agenda hoping, with the help of her staff, to generate some great family and community involvement ideas.*

Definition

Community and family involvement is simple to define. The intent of criteria around these topics is to enrich the program by including the resources and support of the community and families and ensuring an atmosphere of partnership among program staff and families.

Significance

The intent of the standards around community and family involvement are to ensure that the program does not isolate itself from the broader community. Instead, a program should operate as an active part of the community, partner with families and other resources to provide the best care and experience for children, and incorporate rich resources from diverse sources in the community.

A program functioning in isolation from the broader community and providing care and learning for children without partnering with families will be unable to achieve the highest levels of quality care. That program would miss out on rich and meaningful experiences for the children and would not have open and collaborative communication with parents—two things that clearly should happen in the highest quality programs. Programs that understand the value of both relationships benefit immensely. Whether the involvement is through simple things such as materials donations or parent volunteers, or significant things such as a family council that supports the program or a community-sponsored playground, the relationship benefits all. The expectation, however, is not to develop an elaborate community partnership nor to allow families to manage the program. The intent is to increase collaboration and partnerships to ensure that all parties vested in the development and well-being of children are working together. Program staff often get anxious about these criteria, particularly the community-focused criteria. But you need not worry, the expectations are easily achievable, and often programs are much closer to meeting them than they think they are.

Evaluation

While community and family relationships share a lot of commonalities, they are separate and have unique elements. So we will discuss them as distinct relationships with overlapping experiences whenever relevant. This can be true of many third-party quality endorsement system categories; while distinct, one can't function at its best without the others.

Many of the criteria and standards regarding family and community involvement are consistent across third-party quality endorsement systems. The following are examples:

ECERS 38–5.4: Variety of alternatives used to encourage family involvement in children's program.
(Harms, Clifford, and Cryer 2005, 64)

NAEYC 7.A.12: The program facilitates opportunities for families to meet with one another on a formal and informal basis, work together on projects to support the program, and learn from and provide support for each other.
(NAEYC 2005c, 57)

NAC D4: Parents are encouraged to participate in the center's program. Staff members find ways to involve working parents in their child's weekday experience that do not necessarily require time away from their job.
(NAC 2007, 44)

Although the language varies, all of these criteria share the basic intent to ensure families have opportunities to become involved in the program. This is just one of the common categories found in the related criteria. Typically the criteria are aimed at meeting the following goals: partnership, communication, and diversity.

Partnership

A partnership with families promotes a common purpose and helps ensure that families and the program put their efforts toward what is best and relevant for the children. Parents and guardians are the first and most important teachers for their children, and programs must recognize this. Programs have the opportunity to complement this teaching with purposeful and intentional experiences and opportunities for children that families may not be aware of, know the importance of, or be able to provide. Bringing these influences together increases the positive impact on the child.

Community partnerships are intended to ensure the center accesses the resources the community has to offer. This doesn't mean the director has to attend chamber of commerce meetings or sit on a city board. Rather, it simply means being a good and participatory neighbor and exposing children to the diversity and resources found in a community. Partnering with the local library can teach children about this valuable resource, increase their exposure to different types of books, and perhaps spark a lifelong love of reading. Offering to provide children's activities at a community event will help you develop relationships with local families and businesses and send a message to the children in your program of community responsibility and giving back. These partnership examples are simple yet potentially powerful in the messages and learning they provide for children.

Communication

More communication! Better communication! These are often the comments and requests made by families on annual surveys. But what do they mean? Everyone has a different idea of what good communication is. Even when families choose to enroll their child in a learning program, they still want to be a part of their child's day. Many parents and guardians are apart from their children for as many as ten hours a day. Families simply want to understand what's happening during those hours and be a part of their children's lives. Knowing this and knowing that each family has different levels of need can help programs develop and provide effective sources of communication. For example, posting what the class did during the day will allow families to prompt meaningful conversations with their children. So, instead of this exchange:

> Family member: *"What did you do today?"*
> Child: *"I don't know."*

the conversation might sound more like this:

> Family member: *"Tell me about the collage you made today."*
> Child: *"I had red and blue paper and shiny foil. I sticked it on and cut shapes."*

Daily information about eating, napping, mood, and diapering is also vital for families. For example, if their child is easily frustrated all evening and the family doesn't realize the child did not nap, the parenting response may not match the behavior of the child.

Individual and specific information about what the child accomplished, enjoyed, or discovered cannot be underrated. An e-mail with a picture, a note describing an accomplishment or event that sparked interest and joy, or a comment about a new friend or silly quote, are simple but powerful ways to partner with families and provide a meaningful glimpse into their child's day.

Community communication is less common but also valuable. Many opportunities can be found to establish positive community relationships:

- Communicate directly with the city council to ensure the program's needs and insight are considered when new initiatives are on the table.
- Communicate with local schools about school schedules and kindergarten readiness expectations.

- Become involved at the state level as the state develops a quality rating system.
- Participate in the local AEYC.
- Post information about community resources and events in your program for parents to see.

Done well, such efforts will be ongoing and reciprocal, ensuring that the commitment of time and effort needed from the program will be well worth it in the end.

Diversity

Diversity can and should be a part of each aspect of an early childhood program. Diversity or multicultural inclusion should not be an isolated learning experience but rather reflected in all aspects of the program. *Diversity* doesn't just mean *different* or *other*. Considering diversity in an early childhood program should mean considering the differences that exist among families in the program across a broad range of categories: tradition, culture, gender, ethnicity, family structure, and ability. Wider community or world diversity should be represented as well under the same categories.

Respecting and valuing the diversity in your program will shape your partnerships and communication in positive ways. This is often easier than you may think:

- Enhance your dramatic play area with military uniforms, if you are in a military community.
- Ask a Native American community leader to speak at a staff meeting.
- Invite a female athlete to read in your program.
- Provide a holiday lunch instead of a Christmas event.
- Ask the children to create books about their families and display them in the class library.

Although store-bought items such as play food, posters, and dolls can be useful as representational objects, incorporating the diversity found in your own program is more useful. Many programs fail to effectively reflect diversity because staff members define diversity only as cultural or ethnic differences, and they hesitate to ask or admit their lack of knowledge for fear of offending. However, if strong, open family and community partnerships and methods of communication are established, your program can benefit from those relationships and use those resources to strengthen its representation of diversity. Looking to the families and your community is the best way to learn about what true diversity is. Many of the suggestions that follow will help you do that.

Implementation

Increasing and enhancing family and community involvement can often be accomplished through small additions or changes to the program's practices. While big initiatives can get the job done, they are often not necessary. When considering potential actions, think about the following topics and ideas.

Family Connection

FAMILY QUESTIONNAIRES

Beyond the endorsement system questionnaires or surveys, asking families to share some details about themselves, their traditions, and their hobbies is a useful way to get to know each family and to respect and reflect their diverse perspectives in your program. You can introduce a new family to your program in a positive way by sending the message that you value each family as unique. See the Family Questionnaire in appendix C to help you get started.

DAILY NOTES

Be sure your program, at a minimum, sends home a daily note for younger children and a weekly note for preschool and older children (although daily is still preferable). This practice requires a time commitment from teachers, but the response is well worth it. Comment on routine care events, such as napping, eating, and diapering or toileting practice, as well as personal individualized information about the child's day. This is also an ideal place to record a child's learning or discovery. Clearly teachers can't record everything each child did, but mentioning a child's delight in a certain discovery or an anecdote about something they said will give families a glimpse into their child's day and increase the connection between home and school.

CLASSROOM NOTES

A classroom note is helpful too. For children of all ages (except infants), posting and following schedules, with some flexibility, is important—but giving some depth to the schedule is also meaningful. For example, the schedule says outdoor time and the daily classroom note mentions that the children painted with water and large brushes on the sidewalks and discovered how the sun dried their creations.

Mailboxes

Each child needs a place to put things to take home, whether a slot, a folder, a mailbox, or a cubby. Not only can teachers leave things there that should go home, but also if used consistently, the director can count on this place as an established source of communication for important announcements or family notices. Parents or guardians will also come to rely on it, automatically looking there for any information to come home. Children can also put items there that they feel are important, allowing them to support the home/school connection as well.

A separate classroom mailbox for teachers is important too. In the rush of the morning or evening, parents often don't have the time they need to share information. A classroom mailbox allows families to leave messages for teachers and their children if they wish.

E-mail

E-mail is an important method of communication that is often overlooked in child care. Sending a quick note or picture to a parent during the day is a great way to strengthen the relationship. Families often see children only at drop-off and pick-up times. Parents appreciate an opportunity to see their children actively engaged during the day and will increase their support and commitment to their children's early care and learning experience.

Face-to-Face Time

Nothing can take the place of face-to-face communication. Welcoming each child and parent to the classroom each day is important. It sends the message that "You belong here and we're happy to see you." Families understand that staff members are busy with many responsibilities, but a distracted and busy teacher at drop-off time may cause parents to wonder whether their children will get the attention they deserve throughout the day. Body language often communicates stronger messages than spoken words do, so make sure your teachers know this and are aware of their communication style.

Classroom Journal

Ensuring that teachers communicate with each other is also essential to making face-to-face communication work. Nothing is more aggravating than picking up your child, hearing that something happened, asking the teacher about it, and getting the response "I don't know. I wasn't here." If teachers aren't expected to communicate with each other as they pass responsibility for a group of children on to one another, how can they provide the care the children need? The answer is, they can't. The care will be disjointed and families and children will suffer. If teachers do not have the opportunity to verbally exchange information about each child during a shift change, then a journal can give them the opportunity to do so in writing. Jotting down quick notes such as "Franco fell on the playground today—small scrape—cried a minute—lots of TLC—okay" or "Jessie's grandma is picking up today. On approved list," will help immensely.

The Little Things

In all of these methods the family/center partnership should be respected. Program staff should not share information because they have to but because they know it's best for the children. They should also never assume the role of the family by deciding whether or not the parent or guardian should be told something. Simply asking family members what communication methods they prefer and honoring those will be a huge step in the right direction. Phone calls during the day to give them a heads-up about a scraped knee or milestone accomplished help establish an ongoing partnership. Regular announcements about changes in teaching staff, new menus, or center events that may affect the families are important. Put on your parent lens as you evaluate the communication in your center. Communication, down to simple signs telling parents where the class is when not in their room, should not be undervalued.

Newsletters

A monthly newsletter highlighting program and individual classroom events encourages families to get to know what is happening in the whole program rather than just in their child's classroom. Programs can focus on a family of the month or highlight different families to help facilitate community at the center.

Portfolios

An ongoing collection of children's work is an important way for parents and teachers alike to see a child's growth and development. If the program does not already have an expectation for creating and maintaining child portfolios, it is important to develop one (see Collecting Evidence to Show Development over Time, page 166). Compiling portfolios will take up some of the teachers' time but the value comes back to the program and families tenfold.

CONFERENCES

Scheduled and focused meetings for families and teachers to discuss a child's growth and development are an integral part of any high-quality program. Some conferences could also include children, allowing them to be a part of this important discussion.

A conference is often perceived as an event where the teacher tells the family about their child's progress, interests, and daily work. What about looking at it more as a dialogue between partners? If the family members, teacher, and child sit down to share information, ideas, and thoughts about how to support the child's growth and development as an ongoing process instead of an achievement, the conversation will have a very different and collaborative tone. This kind of conversation is even more important if the child has any learning or behavior challenges. A collaborative partnership approach is key.

OPEN-DOOR POLICY

An open-door policy is essential for good communication. Ensuring that parents can visit or observe their child whenever they want and also speak to their caregivers at unscheduled times fosters a trusting and balanced partnership.

FAMILY COUNCIL

Are there opportunities for families to contribute to the program? Could a group of family members meet monthly to plan events such as an end-of-year picnic, clothing and toy drive, or teacher appreciation week? Making it clear up front that the council is not about changing program policy but about supporting the program will establish the intent of the council and alleviate potential disagreements.

REGULAR SURVEYS

Make sure that parents have a regular opportunity to provide anonymous (if they choose) feedback. Typically only the happiest or unhappiest parents are vocal. But what about the rest? Giving families this opportunity and responding to their feedback is an integral component in a positive partnership. See the Family Survey in appendix C for a sample form.

Connecting Families

Families benefit not only from an increased level of communication with the program but also from communication with one another. Approaches might include

- highlighting a family of the month;
- connecting existing families with new families as a reference or even as a mentor/greeter;
- sharing family information in newsletters or a family bulletin board;
- having a shared resources bulletin board;
- pulling together for a specific need (for example, letting families know that one of the program's parents has deployed and the spouse at home needs some support, that a family has welcomed a new baby, or that a family is providing a community service, such as pet sitting, and so on).

Families as Volunteers

If your program functions as a co-op or has a required parent volunteer commitment, you are one step ahead. If your program does not already follow this practice, there's no reason you couldn't start it. Ask family members to collect items for prop boxes, ask volunteers to prepare materials for projects such as cutting shapes or laminating items, send home torn books with a parent to repair spines and pages with book tape, or ask adults to visit the classroom and read a story. These are all small but important contributions.

Parents as Speakers at Meetings

Parents are often powerful guest speakers at staff meetings. For example, we've heard of programs inviting a parent of a newborn to speak about how it felt to drop off their child with "strangers," a parent who is a cartoonist to teach about art, and a parent who is a nurse to talk about allergies. The opportunities are endless and family members are often more than willing. Parents can also help each other. For example, a parent who is an investment broker could offer a workshop on saving for future expenses such as braces or college. A parent who is a health practitioner could offer a workshop on illness prevention. Using these available and free resources can also help meet your other goals of building community and partnerships.

Program Events

Family events such as a pancake breakfast, children's art show, holiday social, community health fair, or programwide participation in a walk-a-thon provide opportunities to strengthen relationships while increasing a sense of community and allowing parents to contribute to this important aspect of their children's lives. Planning and organizing events like these are great ways to use the talents of a family council; the center director doesn't have to do it all. But remember the needs of your diverse families and the developmental stages of the children involved. Asking children to sit for hours watching a holiday program does not take their attention span into consideration. Having a family party celebrating the new year where children sing and dance to their favorite songs does.

Holidays

By using the family questionnaires you can ensure that your holiday celebrations are respectful and inclusive. Hearts and shamrocks are cute decorations but they don't inherently teach the child anything. On the other hand, a cooking project or ethnic game shared by a family will. Choose wisely and consider your families' and children's needs throughout the year. Challenging your own assumptions and habits will strengthen the learning opportunities you provide.

It's as simple as that. Family involvement in your program does not have to be elaborate, time consuming, or stressful. Rather it should be a seamless partnership that enhances the program and is a natural part of each day.

Community Involvement

Community involvement is equally as simple. What follows are a few approaches to ensure it is effective as well.

Community Field Trips

Bringing children out to the community or even bringing the community to the children is a great way to make a connection. In *Solutions for Early Childhood Directors* (2003), Kathy Lee suggests visiting local businesses, such as a bakery or nursing home, where the children can meet new people, develop skills, and build their own relationships and connections. Other places such as the library, the fire department, the community center, a county park, restaurants, a local gardening center, the bank, or even the grocery store are great learning opportunities as well. Lee encourages taking pictures and sending copies to the business after the event so they too can enjoy the long-term benefit of the field trip. Field trips don't have to be to elaborate places like water slides or amusement parks. While fun, such trips are not focused on development and learning (and sometimes safety). The community is rich with resources. And there are an equal number of opportunities to bring the "field trip" to the children by asking guests to visit the program.

Be sure to show appreciation for any and all involvement. This is important practice for children to learn and extends the learning and impact of the experience. Sending children's art (relevant to the experience or not) as a token of appreciation, child-written thank-you notes, or pictures will be immensely appreciated by anyone who shares their talents with your program. For example, think how amazing it would be for a child to walk into a bank they toured with their class and see their artwork displayed on the wall.

COMMUNITY TRAINERS

We discussed taking advantage of family members as speakers or trainers at meetings—community members could provide the same service. Many community members will be happy to oblige for the potential marketing opportunity it affords them. Maybe a local dentist will share tips on preparing children for their first visit or a hardware store owner will offer a workshop for parents and children. Tap into the rich resources of local colleges—dental students, for example, may be eager to support the program and may even get school credit. Consider, too, the chamber of commerce or city Web sites.

COMMUNITY EVENTS

Stay abreast of community events and participate whenever possible. Being visible and contributing, whether at a local fair or a walk-a-thon, is good role modeling for the children and develops the reputation of the program in a positive way.

COMMUNITY VOLUNTEERS

Similar to family volunteers, community volunteers can be very helpful. For example, one center had residents from a local assisted-living community make bibs for their program. It saved money for the program and helped the assisted-living residents and families bond with the children's families. We've also seen college athletes, city mayors, and a police chief visit as guest readers. Get creative—perhaps a local garden center or florist will help you plant a garden for the children, or a fitness center may offer a free parent/child class. Keep safety in mind always, but realize that community volunteers provide unique experiences for the children and their families.

COMMUNITY RESOURCES

All early childhood programs can benefit from donated supplies, whether from a cost-saving perspective, a need for open-ended materials, a desire to support recycling or reuse efforts, or all three. Finding these resources in your community is easier than you might think. Stop by a local frame shop and ask for mat board remnants. Go to a hardware store and ask for any left-over carpet pieces, plastic piping, or other building supplies. Visit a camping store and ask about retired models of miniature tents. Go to a film processing shop and collect unused film canisters, and so on.

LITTLE CONVENIENCES

Partnering with the community should be fun and rewarding. It can also make parents' lives easier. Can the local dry cleaner provide a drop-off at your program? Can a hairdresser provide haircuts for children in the mornings? Make use of early childhood, social, and school resources. If the district provides free health, hearing, or other screenings, figure out how to include them in your program. If social service organizations support children with learning or behavior challenges, work to develop a relationship. It is crucial for many children that you take that step.

SHARE YOUR RESOURCES

Don't just look at how you can benefit from the community—consider how you can contribute to the strength of the community. Can you speak at an event? Can you share your space for community events or meetings? Can you hold a bake sale or a read-a-thon to raise money for a community cause?

PEN PALS

A great way for children to develop literacy skills is to use those skills in a practical situation. Writing letters, reading letters, and overall two-way communication through print are valuable lessons that can be even more meaningful if children learn about or connect with someone new in the community. While we have been referring to the community as a local entity, in this case it can also be a broader world community. Children could be pen pals with a child care program in a different locale (urban to rural, southern to northern, beach to plains), another state, or another country.

These are just some of the opportunities that exist. There are, of course, many more ways to include families and the community in your program. The important thing is to consider all possibilities as opportunities rather than as obligations—a practice that will enrich the program and the children's learning and will help you create a thriving and respected program that is a integral part of the community.

As easy as building these relationships may sound, it is still a challenge to find the time to do so, especially if it is a new practice. Making a monthly commitment is the best way to take the steps required to build these partnerships.

 ## PROVE IT SUGGESTIONS

Family and Community Involvement

Commit to monthly or quarterly family and community activities such as the following:

May

Family Connection: plant the center garden

Community Connection: ask for donations for center garden, send photos and thank-you cards from children afterward

First Quarter

Family Activity: schedule a parents' night out and provide child care on a Friday

Community Activity: plan a field trip to a local assisted-living community; ask residents to read to children

Keep evidence such as flyers, pictures, letters, journals, documentation boards, and more to ensure the long-term benefits of these activities are enjoyed. While you may first engage in this concerted effort just to meet third-party quality endorsement system standards, planning monthly connections should develop into a long-term habit. Plan and post your commitments on a bulletin board to remind yourself of their importance. Soon it will be second nature to consider families and the community in your planning.

Refer to the Family and Community Activity Planning Sheet in appendix C for a blank form to help you plan your ideas for the year.

Sunshine Child Development Center

At the staff meeting, many staff members offered ideas for community and family involvement. Martha was glad to have involved the entire staff since they had some fresh and creative ideas and even volunteered to help plan and organize some of the events. For example, Shondra shared that a grandmother of one of her toddlers offered to sew blankets or other items for the center. Magda offered to ask her sister, who works at a local bank, if they would like to display some of the children's artwork in their display case. Martha left the meeting with a whole list of simple ideas to involve her families and become a more active member of the community. She felt these would make a positive impact right away. Some staff members offered to create a bulletin board the next day highlighting their accreditation activities.

Part 4
What's Next?

You've finished the self-study, you've submitted the paperwork to request an on-site assessment visit, and you're ready. So, now what?

It often takes a few months before representatives from the third-party quality endorsement system show up for the final assessment, and the waiting stage can be as nerve wracking as the self-study. Maintaining the high levels of quality you achieved is a challenge unto itself, and it is easy to lose the intense focus you had during the self-study. The next two chapters will focus on how to keep that flame alive now and continuing on well after receiving your endorsement results.

The On-Site Assessment Visit

Martha and Georgia, her assistant director, are thrilled! Yesterday they made a special trip to the post office to mail their NAC submission paperwork. Today they are sitting in Martha's office when Georgia asks, "So, what are we doing today?"

Martha thinks for a moment and says, "Well, I guess we could . . . um, I honestly don't know. It seems like we've done everything. All our action plans are done, our classrooms look great, the teachers have never been better, and our document collection is finished."

Georgia shifts uncomfortably in her chair and asks disbelievingly, "Could it be we have nothing left to do?"

How would you answer that question?

If your answer is "No, there is always something that needs to be done," then you are on the right track. You and Martha are in the waiting phase when there is plenty to do to prepare for the visit. Your focus during the self-study has been on raising the level of quality in your program, and now you have the unique opportunity to subtly shift that focus to the actual visit. (Although our goal is not to teach to the test, it is still valuable to take the time to be fully prepared for it.)

Preparing for the Visit

One of the many reasons for completing the self-study is to raise the level of care and education your program provides to the children, and you have seen those improvements manifest themselves over the course of the last few months. The self-study is an exciting, interesting, and fulfilling process in itself, with many tangible benefits to all the key stakeholders in your program. A secondary goal to completing a detailed self-study is to prepare for the on-site assessment visit. If every step of the self-study has been carefully and thoroughly completed, then your program is ready for the assessment. However, the representatives of the third-party quality endorsement system do not show up on your doorstep the day after you have completed the self-study. Typically, a period of weeks or months goes by before the visit happens. Your challenge is to use this time for meaningful and focused work that will maintain both the enthusiasm generated throughout the self-study and the high levels of quality attained.

Here are ten things to consider in preparing for your third-party quality endorsement system's on-site assessment visit:

1. How will the third-party quality endorsement system communicate with me regarding the visit?
2. How are visits scheduled?
3. Will I know the exact date of the visit, or is there a visit window?
4. What does the third-party quality endorsement system's representative actually do during the visit?
5. What is the role of the center management during the visit?
6. What is expected of the teachers on that day?
7. What documentation will the representative want to see?
8. Does my third-party quality endorsement system have specific requirements for how they want to review evidence of compliance with the standards and criteria?
9. What should I be doing to prepare the staff for the visit?
10. What should I be doing to prepare myself for the visit?

Many third-party quality endorsement systems will send you some guidance regarding these topics after you have submitted your request for an on-site visit. Others will give you access to specific people in their organization who can answer your questions. Yet others leave you to figure it out on your own. Regardless of how the third-party quality endorsement system functions in this regard, it is *your* responsibility to research these things to make sure that your program is completely ready.

Let's take a look at some best practices for preparing for an on-site visit.

Communicate with the Third-Party Quality Endorsement System

At this stage of the process you will probably have had some contact with the third-party quality endorsement organization. Many organizations have dedicated people who help programs in the on-site visit stage of their self-studies.

☑ PROVE IT ACTIVITY #23

Contact Information

Take the time to find the following information.

Name of the organization: _____

_____

Contact person(s): _____

_____

Telephone number(s): _____

_____

E-mail address(es): _____

_____

Best way to communicate with the contact(s): _____

_____

After determining who to talk to, decide what still needs clarification. Your self-study materials may contain a wealth of information regarding the on-site visit, and your first task is to read all of it. If you're still unsure about a few things, make a note of them below.

_____

_____

_____

_____

_____

_____

Check in with your contact person and ask your questions. Write down the answers you receive, along with the name of the person you spoke to, and the date of your conversation. If you send an e-mail, save the response e-mail for your reference and as proof of your communication.

Keep the Teaching Staff Focused

Set the expectation that the high levels of quality achieved during the self-study need to be maintained until the on-site visit and beyond. For now, the best way is to set short-term goals and tasks that teachers can focus on, giving them the opportunity to practice and hone their skills. Break down the things you want them to focus on for the next several weeks or months, and create some weekly project-style tasks around these. Preparing Teachers for the On-Site Visit #1, Preparing Teachers for the On-Site Visit #2, Preparing Teachers for the On-Site Visit #3 in appendix D provide some ready-to-use projects.

New Staff Orientation

Have a plan for introducing new staff to the third-party quality endorsement system and the expectations attached to the process. Ensuring that this is part of their orientation will get them on track from the start and minimize any discrepancies in the care and education offered in your program.

Walk Your Program on a Daily Basis

The best way to know what's going on in your program is to be knee-deep in it. Think like a validator, and walk your program daily. Look for signs of success and acknowledge and reward them. Note the areas of opportunity and work on those as quickly as possible. Being an on-the-spot manager will keep your standards high and everybody's eyes on the prize. Refer to the Daily Walkabout Sheet in appendix D. Use it as you walk your program and focus on the specific points listed. Then create a quick action plan to ensure that you address areas of opportunity on a daily basis.

Get Organized

It is in your best interests to be as organized as you can possibly be. As the leader of your team, you are the role model for everyone else. If you are organized, prepared, and calm, the others will be too.

 **PROVE IT ACTIVITY #24**

Get Organized Checklist

Look around your office and ask yourself these questions:

☐ Is your filing up to date?

☐ Can you locate any document within thirty seconds?

☐ Have you collected all the documents that the third-party quality endorsement system's representative will need to review?

☐ Are these organized in a logical way?

☐ Are staff members' and children's files complete?

☐ Do you have a "Plan B" should any teacher be ill on the day of the visit?

☐ Do you know for certain that each teacher is prepared for the visit? Are they prepared for an interview with the representative of the third-party quality endorsement system?

☐ Are you ready for an exit interview, should the third-party quality endorsement system require one?

If you answered *no* to any of these questions, you know where to focus your energies. Don't panic! Take one situation at a time, make a plan to get it done, and then do it. At this point you are a master of creating and executing plans, so don't abandon that well-practiced skill now.

Talk to an Expert

Guess what? Yours is not the first program to go through this process. That means other people out there have insights as to what an on-site visit is all about. If you have access to center directors who have been through this process, now is the time to pick their brains. If you don't know anyone within your own circle of colleagues or acquaintances, here's how to find someone.

Go back to Prove It Activity #5. Among the marketing and enrollment reasons for pursuing a third-party quality endorsement you listed center administrators who had already achieved an endorsement for their programs. Contact them again and reintroduce yourself. Whether you have old or new experts at hand, invite them to your center. Show off your classrooms, ask their opinions, and pick their brains about what occurred during their on-site visits. Ask them for a "top five" list of things to be aware of, and talk about the exit interview if there was one.

The On-Site Assessment Visit

Each third-party quality endorsement system has unique requirements for its on-site visit, but they share several commonalities.

- A representative of the third-party quality endorsement system will be on-site to review how well your program measures up to its standards and criteria.
- The representative's responsibility is to record how well the program meets the standards and criteria, not how well the children behave that day.
- The representative will observe a selection, if not all, of your classrooms.
- The representative will be looking for a variety of evidence that clearly shows that your program meets the standards and criteria of the endorsement.
- The evidence could be in the form of observed actions, evaluated environments, documentation, or staff interviews.
- The representative will review operational policies and procedures as described in the third-party quality endorsement system's standards and criteria.
- Any occurrences of serious breaches in licensing regulations during the on-site visit will most likely result in a suspended visit.
- There will probably be some form of an exit interview, either to discuss the findings of the visit or the processes and procedures of the visit.

Exit and Teacher Interviews

Some third-party quality endorsement system representatives conclude their visit with an exit interview. Most exit interviews include a review of the day, including assurances that all procedures were accurately followed. Typically, any significant issues or concerns are addressed at this time. Some representatives also include time to discuss the findings of the visit, and the center director may have an opportunity to respond.

The representative is there to record what they observe, not make assumptions or decisions. If you find yourself in the position of responding to an unmet criteria you should explain without defending. For example, if the representative indicates that she did not observe children washing their hands before using the sensory table, your response should *not* be this:

That has never happened before. We always pass our licensing visits.

Instead, your response could be:

We provide training for all staff on hand washing upon hire. Hand-washing policies and procedures are posted in all classrooms. We will ensure hand washing is reviewed at our next staff meeting.

By responding this way those who review the visit results will know what you do now and what you plan do to address this situation. They would not understand that from the first statement.

At the time of the exit interview, or in the mail after the visit, the representative may provide the center director with an assessment or review of the process. It is important to complete this form. It does not affect your results in any way, but does provide the third-party quality endorsement system with valuable information to continue improving their system and will, in the event of a complaint, support your argument if you feel the eventual decision is inaccurate.

Occasionally, representatives may interview teachers. If the third-party quality endorsement system uses this method its materials will say so. Teachers should be prepared to intelligently discuss their classroom—which is sometimes easier said than done. Practice makes perfect. Ask teachers to spend time practicing responses to classroom criteria questions such as these:

- "What is your approach to behavior guidance?"
- "How do you support literacy development?"
- "What large-motor opportunities do you provide indoors?"

Practicing responses to such questions may feel awkward but will help teachers feel much more prepared on the day of the visit. The Daily Walkabout Sheet in appendix D offers suggestions for practice questions.

Reacting to the Results

Responding appropriately to the on-site visit decision is crucial. Whether it's good news or not, your program's response (in both words and actions) is important in maintaining the momentum you created during the self-study. Good news doesn't mean the work is over—quite the opposite actually. Maintaining the high level of quality achieved during the process for a sustained period of time is the biggest challenge.

Conversely, bad news doesn't mean all is lost. Sometimes bad news is very informative and, if considered as such, can be instrumental in leading the program toward long-term success.

Accreditation

If your program pursued a national accreditation, the results could be one of the following: accredited, deferred/pending, or denied.

ACCREDITED

Your program has met enough of the standards and criteria to fulfill the requirements for accreditation for that organization. You will enjoy your accredited status for a specific number of years, during which you must submit an annual report describing any changes and improvements to your program. You may also be subject to an unannounced evaluation visit during this time to ensure you are still maintaining the expectations of the endorsement system.

DEFERRED/PENDING

Your program has met most of the standards and criteria required by the accreditation organization but your evidence was insufficient for a few key factors. The accreditation organization is giving you an opportunity to submit this missing evidence within a certain period of time. If what you submit is acceptable, you will then have fulfilled the expectations of the accreditation organization and receive accreditation. In some cases, the accreditation organization may do another on-site visit of your program to assess the evidence of compliance with their standards and criteria. After receiving accreditation, you must submit an annual report describing any changes and improvements to your program throughout your accreditation term.

DENIED

Your program did not provide sufficient evidence that it is meeting a significant number of accreditation standards and criteria. It is possible that accreditation was denied due to a significant event that happened during the on-site visit, such as a breach of licensing regulations.

If accreditation is denied, the accreditation organization typically sends a report outlining the standards and criteria that were not met and recommendations for program improvement. You will be advised to redo the self-study process and to reapply for a visit when the new self-study is complete. If you feel that accreditation was unfairly denied, the accreditation organization usually has an appeals process whereby you can state your case for a second review of the on-site visit findings. The appeals process decision is final, and if accreditation is denied, then you will need to restart the self-study process.

Rating System

If your program pursued an environment rating scale (ERS) or a quality rating system (QRS), the results are typically in the form of a rating on a scale. In this type of third-party quality endorsement system, your program cannot fail per se, but is awarded a specific spot on that scale. Many states have "star" or "step" rating systems, and your program can attain any number of stars depending on how well it meets the requirements of that system. The rating systems with their points, grades, or stars are as many and as varied as there are states participating in such systems, so it is beneficial for you to research what each grade or rating means to your center. Sometimes the highest level is not achievable due to things like staff qualifications or ratios, but a slightly lower level still indicates high quality. In some cases, achieving national accreditation can result in a program automatically receiving the highest rating in a state quality rating system. You should research the levels and what they mean and what other local high-quality centers are achieving.

Whether you participated in an ERS or another kind of quality rating system, it is important to interpret what your rating means. For example, if you pursued a system with a rating scale of 1 thru 5 (1 being the lowest acceptable rating, and 5 the highest) and you achieved an overall rating of 3, then it is evident you have further to go. However, the next level may include a component beyond your control, such as building design, in which case you'll have to decide whether your program will benefit from further effort. Celebrate your success of achieving the score you did and what that means in terms of growth and accomplishment in your program; then turn your eye toward that next level.

The third-party quality endorsement system typically sends a report describing what your results mean and what your areas of opportunity are—a valuable document for planning your next steps. The on-site assessment should highlight program areas where you need to concentrate your efforts in the months ahead. This report often breaks down the areas of opportunity into the classrooms where they were most evident or into the overall areas of competencies around which the standards and criteria are organized. Such detailed information points out the first step in continuing the journey to maintain the levels of quality achieved.

Maintaining Quality Standards

Sunshine Child Development Center

The mail arrived a few minutes ago, and Georgia notices a letter from NAC in the pile. Grabbing it, she rushes down the hallway to find Martha. It's been eleven weeks since their on-site visit, and they have been anxiously waiting for this missive. "Martha, look! I think our results are here," says Georgia as she catches her breath. Martha stops what she's doing, gingerly takes the letter from Georgia, and says, "Let's open this in my office."

Once there, Martha tears open the envelope and unfolds the letter. Her eyes quickly skim over the page looking for the magic words.

"Well?" asks Georgia. Martha looks at her, feeling a little choked up.

"Georgia," she whispers, "we did it!"

One of the many reasons for pursuing a third-party quality endorsement is to raise the level of quality in your program for the children, their families, and your staff. The benefits of this endorsement are many. Keeping a program running at these high levels of quality can be challenging, especially if you consider that these levels need to be permanently maintained. Programs often view the award of the endorsement as the last step in the quality process. But it's really the beginning.

If your program achieves accreditation, you will receive a report outlining your areas of success. The accreditation organizations assume that these levels of quality will be at the very least maintained throughout the accreditation term. The report will also list the areas of opportunity that still exist in your program, and the accreditation organization will assume that you will work to improve these areas throughout the accreditation term. You will need to submit an annual report to the accreditation organization on the maintenance and improvement tasks you have undertaken. Clearly, you can't simply hang up the accreditation certificate, file the decision report, and call it done.

If your program pursued an ERS of some sort, then the graded results will indicate its strengths and weaknesses. These third-party quality endorsement systems also expect you to undertake plans to maintain your program's high scores and further improve in any areas having lower scores.

In either case, the final grade or decision is your prompt to start maintaining and improving upon the high level of care and education your program achieved during your initial self-study. In this chapter we focus on some practical ways to do this.

Getting on Track

Your on-site visit is over, your stress levels have significantly dropped, and if you are one of the lucky ones (well prepared and hard working) like Martha and her center, you have received your third-party quality endorsement. Phew! But, as you well know, the real work of ensuring that your center continues to have a high level of program quality is only just beginning. How have you been doing so far?

 **PROVE IT ACTIVITY #25**

Post-Endorsement Quiz

Take this quiz to help you figure out how well you've been doing since achieving your third-party quality endorsement.

Observations	Yes	No	Don't Know
1. I still have the same staff as during the on-site visit.			
2. My teachers are showing further progress with their professional development toward meeting the educational qualifications.			
3. My assistant teachers/aides are showing further progress with their professional development toward meeting the educational qualifications.			

Observations	Yes	No	Don't Know
4. The classrooms are developmentally appropriate and include • real-life pictures and props; • an interesting and diverse selection of children's books; • items depicting multiculturalism and diversity, as appropriate for the age of the children; • displays of children's work at their eye level; • information for parents about classroom events, the curriculum, and their child's progress; • interesting, fun, and appropriate learning centers for the children; • a learning environment that is sufficiently enriched by the classroom teacher; • a balance of child- and teacher-initiated activities.			
5. We continue to display high levels of cleanliness in the center.			
6. Our safety practices are still consistent with the standards and criteria.			
7. My teaching staff responds to both the children's and families' needs.			
8. Teacher-child interactions are caring, courteous, and encourage open-ended dialogue at the child's level.			
9. Classroom teachers regularly observe and assess children in a natural setting.			
10. Daily evidence shows that the educational goals of my program are being met in each classroom. The teaching staff visibly provide many opportunities for the children to investigate, question, discover, problem solve, and take initiative.			
11. Children are happy, engaged, and interact with their learning environment, other children, and adults in the center. Teaching staff clearly guide and assist children in reaching this goal.			

Staying on Track

As an integral part of maintaining your center's high quality, regularly review the endorsement standards and criteria. If you discover evidence of "slipping," you must take immediate corrective action. An effective way to do this is to follow a simple three-step process: observe, take action, and follow up.

Observe

Create checklists of standards and criteria around specific topics such as curriculum, interactions, health and safety, and so on. Provide one checklist at a time to all teaching staff. At least once a month, observe the center's activities using these checklists. Note any deficiencies or slipping standards.

Take Action

Create manageable action plans based on the results of these observations. Be sure to include deadlines in your plans. Provide individual feedback to any staff members participating in the plan. Be specific and clear about your expectations and the time frame in which you expect the corrections to occur.

Follow Up

Follow up with staff members to ensure the action plan tasks are being corrected as planned. Following up is key to your program's success! Continuous classroom observations and tours by center management will help teaching staff and center management stay focused on the third-party quality endorsement standards and criteria. By requiring your staff to regularly conduct evaluations of themselves and their classrooms, you will keep the quality flame burning in your program. Your goal is to maintain the high levels of quality the program displayed on the day of the on-site visit. You know your program can do it!

Here are some ideas to help you do so:

Use the Tools

Each third-party quality endorsement system has all the lists and tools you could possibly need. Take another look at your self-study materials. Create a schedule over an extended period of time during which you and your teaching staff use the tools and checklists to assess the program's level of quality. Follow the three-step process of observe, take action, and follow up to resolve any issues.

Survey, Survey, Survey!

The best way to find out how you are doing is to ask those who are experiencing and delivering your services. Reuse the Staff Survey and the Family Survey in your third-party quality endorsement system's materials to check how you are doing. Select a random sample of families and staff members and use the survey tools in the self-study materials. Based on the results of these surveys, create a plan (with deadlines) to correct any developing deficiencies.

Introduce the Standards and Criteria to New Staff

Create a plan to introduce the standards and criteria of the third-party quality endorsement system to your new staff members. As you hire new staff members, keep teacher and assistant teacher qualifications in mind. During interviews, discuss the third-party quality endorsement status of the center and the importance of the teachers in maintaining this endorsement. After hiring new employees, introduce the standards and criteria to them and provide them with appropriate training in the system as needed.

Identify Mentors and Trainers

Start slowly. Identify which teachers can mentor the new staff members on the standards and criteria. Check in often with new staff members to make sure their understanding and execution is on the mark. Coach them as needed as they work toward implementing the standards and criteria.

Keep Up the Training

Use every opportunity to train your staff. From staff meetings to community workshops, training is an effective way to broaden and improve their skills. Model what you want to see in classrooms, and use on-the-spot training techniques to ensure that staff members are fulfilling their responsibilities. Stay in touch with everybody's progress toward meeting the professional development requirements, and encourage teachers and assistant teachers to enhance their professional development.

Third-Party Quality Endorsement System Paperwork Requirements

When you received your endorsement results, the documents included instructions on what, if any, annual paperwork is required. Each third-party quality endorsement system is unique in this. To help you know what is needed, complete the form below.

✔ PROVE IT ACTIVITY #26

Post-Endorsement Paperwork Requirements

Name of third-party quality endorsement system: _____

_____

Contact details: _____

_____

Telephone: _____

Fax: _____

E-mail: _____

Expiration date of endorsement: _____

Annual paperwork required: _____ Due date: _____

Annual paperwork required: _____ Due date: _____

Annual paperwork required: _____ Due date: _____

Annual paperwork required: _____ Due date: _____

When to start the self-study for reendorsement: _____

_____

When to submit the paperwork for reendorsement: _____

_____

Enjoying the Benefits

The process of achieving and maintaining high levels of quality is one of the most valuable things you can do in the life of your program—a jolt into consciously remembering why we all entered this field in the first place. While working through the self-study, you can easily get lost in the details of the steps and checklists. But step back on a regular basis to remember the great things that happen in your program during and after the process.

The benefits of achieving a third-party quality endorsement are not short term and go way beyond hanging the certificate of achievement on the wall. The positive outcomes for children are obvious: meaningful learning experiences, extended and appropriate opportunities for growth and development, focused teaching and facilitation, attention to children's individual needs, and the opportunity to play and interact with other children and adults in ways that foster valuable life skills.

Teachers also benefit in many ways. For example, they may obtain additional professional development, stronger teaching skills, a deeper understanding of children and child development, an enjoyable and satisfying work environment, opportunities to learn from their peers, opportunities to connect with the families and their communities, and a professional and well-run work environment.

These positive aspects can also benefit the families in your program as a whole. The value of having families and caregivers on the same page in regard to meeting the children's emotional, social, physical, and cognitive needs cannot be measured. When families place their children in your care, your program becomes an integral part of raising and educating their children. Teachers are viewed as professionals who can contribute to the decisions about each child's care and early education as part of creating an environment for successful and lifelong learning.

If your program and your families achieve these goals and realize these benefits in even a small way, then your job is done—and third-party quality endorsement has helped you find the best possible way for your program to be successful.

It is far from easy, but you should relish that fact. If achieving third-party quality endorsement were easy, everyone would do it. Instead, it is an endeavor that only the best of the best attain, and those programs wholeheartedly embrace the education and development of young children.

Congratulations on your continued success!

Appendix A:
Preparing for the Process

Researching Your Market

Third-Party Quality Endorsement System Information

Learning Styles Quiz

In-Service and Professional Development Planning Chart

Researching Your Market

Make a copy of this page for each center or program you contact.

Center/ Program Name	Contact Phone Numbers/ Web site Address	Contact Name	Endorsement
How long have you had this endorsement?			
Why did you chose this endorsement?			
What benefits do you see in your program from having this endorsement?			
What do your families say about this endorsement?			
What does your staff say about this endorsement?			
Would you choose to use this endorsement process again? Why?			

Third-Party Quality Endorsement System Information

Make a copy of this form for each endorsement you are reviewing.

Name of Third-Party Quality Endorsement System:		
Web site address:		
Phone numbers:		
Costs:		
Materials:		
Training requirements (if any):		
Self-study paperwork submission:		
Site visit:		
Self-study steps:		
Paperwork requirements:		
Recommended length of time for self-study:	Additional previsit requirements:	Licensing status requirements:
Staff education requirements:	Center director/program leader education requirements:	

Third-Party Quality Endorsement System Information (cont.)

Major focus appears to be

- ☐ health and safety
- ☐ curriculum
- ☐ interactions
- ☐ family connections
- ☐ community connections
- ☐ teaching staff
- ☐ administration and general operations
- ☐ facility or building
- ☐ other: _____
- ☐ other: _____

Annual requirements after third-party quality endorsement has been achieved:

- ☐ annual reports
- ☐ costs: _____
- ☐ additional on-site visits: _____
- ☐ possible unscheduled visits: _____
- ☐ required staff training: _____
- ☐ other: _____

Learning Styles Quiz

Visual	Y	N	Auditory	Y	N	Kinesthetic	Y	N
I remember faces well.			I enjoy rhymes and tongue twisters.			I enjoy doing physical activities while thinking through issues or problems.		
I prefer reading to listening to music or watching TV.			I can study and listen to music at the same time.			I fidget and fiddle a lot when I sit for a long time.		
I prefer to sit in the front when in a training room.			I prefer to sit along the sides in a training room.			I don't care where I sit in a training room.		
I love Post-It Notes!			Earphones are the best invention ever!			I like to figure out how things work by taking them apart and putting them back together again.		
I like to draw diagrams to explain a point.			I enjoy listening to people speak, especially when they have a good command of the language.			I like solving riddles and doing jigsaw puzzles.		
I prefer watching movies on the big screen rather than on TV.			I prefer listening to music to reading or watching TV.			I like to assemble and fix things.		
I find myself doodling while I'm listening or talking on the phone.			I hear little sounds that others typically don't.			I notice and appreciate the texture and feel of fabrics, clothes, furniture, and so on.		
I use lists to plan activities and complete tasks.			I remember song lyrics and jingles easily.			I prefer typing to writing with a pen.		
I write things down when I have to remember them.			I remember telephone numbers better if I hear them.			I remember telephone numbers better after I have used them once or twice.		
I am easily distracted by movement.			I am easily distracted by noise.			I am very sensitive to smells.		
Total			**Total**			**Total**		

Key to Learning Styles Quiz Results

The 'Y' column with the highest total indicates your learning style preference.

The 'N' column with the highest total indicates your least favorite learning style.

Your preference: _____

Typically, we all have indicators from each learning style, and *ideally* should have a fair balance of these to be the most effective learners that we can be.

In-Service and Professional Development Planning Chart

Name	Preferred Method	Plan for Achieving	Status

In-Service and Professional Development Planning Chart, with Goals

Version 1

Name	Preferred Method	Plan for Achieving	Status	Goal

Version 2

Name	Goal	Preferred Method	Plan for Achieving	Status

Appendix B:
The Process

Document or Evidence Collection

Timeline Planner

Self-Study Planning and Progress Checklist

Family Action Plan

Staff Training Plan

Classroom Action Plan

Director's Action Plan

Document or Evidence Collection

Developing a system for document and evidence collection from the start is important. Whether you are pursuing a third party quality endorsement system that requires a document review for the administrative and management functions only, or you are pursuing a system that requires classrooms to also collect documents and evidence, it is important to develop this tool from the start. This ensures you have adequate time to understand what you currently meet and what you need to work toward as part of your action plan.

There are many ways to put a document collection system together. The following suggestions are some best practices—things that are not necessarily essential or required components but have served programs well time and again:

- Use a file box or file folder rather than a binder. A binder can limit space for dictation and sometimes influences the design making it more scrapbook-like, losing the intent of the task. Binders can work but users should be cautious. Document or file boxes tend to work better.
- Online systems are possible as well. For example, NAEYC has approved a few organizations for classroom portfolio systems for their portfolio requirements.
- Review the documents required and collect the evidence that is "easy." Then develop a plan for ongoing document development and collection for the more challenging or complex standards.
- Reflect on each required document and determine which evidence best validates or proves your program meets the standard. Completing a form such as the Criteria Evaluation Form (in appendix C) for each document can help both you and the validator understand the rationale behind each piece of evidence. If staff members are also involved in this process, or working on additional evidence boxes, it can help them articulate how they meet each standard, which adds to their professional knowledge.
- Keep the validator in mind when you organize your system. Make it easy for him or her to locate and understand your evidence. Validators have a limited amount of time and often see myriad systems, documents, and evidence. What may seem obvious to you may be a challenge for a validator to understand.
- Label everything with the standard or criterion number it references. If a document serves as evidence for more than one standard or

criterion, make a copy and place it where it belongs. This is much better than "See standard XYZ for documentation . . ."

- If you do not have anything to verify a standard or criterion, then you must add that information to an improvement or action plan, make the necessary changes to your program, and then provide the evidence.

- Photographs can be very useful but need clear dictation next to them to ensure the validator doesn't have to guess why you are using the picture as evidence.

- Remember, as much as a validator might enjoy perusing your document box, there is limited time. Too much evidence can be as big of a challenge as too little. Limit yourself to one to three pieces of evidence per standard or criterion.

- Ask a third party to review your documents to be sure they make sense to an outsider.

- If something is too large to include in a document box, such as an incident log, include a note indicating where the documentation can be found. However, leaving a note saying it is on the wall in a classroom is not acceptable. That type of evidence is used in a classroom observation.

Timeline Planner

Month 1:

_____

_____

_____

_____

_____

Month 2:

_____

_____

_____

_____

_____

Month 3:

_____

_____

_____

_____

_____

Month 4:

_____

_____

_____

_____

_____

Timeline Planner (cont.)

Month 5:

_____

_____

_____

_____

_____

Month 6:

_____

_____

_____

_____

_____

Month 7:

_____

_____

_____

_____

_____

Month 8:

_____

_____

_____

_____

_____

Timeline Planner (cont.)

Month 9:

_____

_____

_____

_____

_____

Month 10:

_____

_____

_____

_____

Month 11:

_____

_____

_____

_____

Month 12:

_____

_____

_____

_____

Timeline Planner (cont.)

Month 13:

_____

_____

_____

_____

_____

Month 14:

_____

_____

_____

_____

_____

Month 15:

_____

_____

_____

_____

_____

Month 16:

_____

_____

_____

_____

_____

Timeline Planner (cont.)

Month 17:

_____

_____

_____

_____

_____

Month 18:

_____

_____

_____

_____

_____

Congratulations, you have just started the self-study!

Self-Study Planning and Progress Checklist

Self-Study Step	Scheduled Date of Completion	Actual Date of Completion	Follow-Up Notes
Third-Party Quality Endorsement System			
1. Select			
2. Order			
3. Read			
Evaluation Task 1 Identify documentation tools (surveys, checklists, observations, evaluations)			
Evaluation Task 2 Assign documentation tasks (determine who completes what paperwork)			
Evaluation Task 3 Complete the first round of documentation tasks			
Planning Task 1 Identify areas of opportunity (create action plans)			
Planning Task 2 Assign action plan items			
Making Improvements Task 1 Create weekly action plans			
Making Improvements Task 2 Complete weekly action plan tasks			
Reevaluating Task 1 Revisit the documentation task list			
Reevaluating Task 2 Review documentation			
Reevaluating Task 3 Revisit your master plan			
Submit Request for On-site Visit			

Family Action Plan

Criteria/ Standards	Action Tasks	People Responsible	Completion Date

Staff Training Plan

Criteria/ Standards	Training Topics	Training Method and Audience	People Responsible	Completion Date

Classroom Action Plan

Classroom: _____

Criteria/ Standards	Improvement Tasks	People Responsible	Completion Date

Director's Action Plan

Criteria/ Standards	Action Tasks	People Responsible	Completion Date

Appendix C: The Content

Developing Policies and Procedures

Physical Environment Quick Check

Health and Safety Checklist

Criteria Evaluation Form

Interactions Self-Quiz

Family Questionnaire

Family Survey

Family and Community Activity Planning Sheet

Developing Policies and Procedures

> Many standards require a program policy or procedure. It is important to develop these with thought and consideration.

Policies

Policies and procedures often go hand in hand. A policy is a rule or guidance and a procedure is how the policy is executed. For example, a program could have a policy to protect children from all allergens. Their procedures may be to ask parents to identify allergies at enrollment, have allergy postings in classrooms, train staff on allergies, remove pets that shed or have dander from the center, and so on. The policies assessed by a third-party quality endorsement system typically cover many different topics. Sometimes it is clear how the policy affects high quality, such as a policy on ethical behavior. Sometimes it is less clear, such as a policy on insurance coverage. While most would not disagree with the need for insurance in early childhood programs, some may ask how it correlates to high quality for children.

There are two lines of reasoning for most required policies and procedures:

1. The policy provides for a safe, stable, and predictable environment that ensures the focus can remain on learning and development. A program without these types of policies will find itself constantly distracted with ancillary issues, family/staff disputes, licensing challenges and the like.

2. Policies that don't have a direct correlation to quality are to ensure the endorsement is truly meaningful and that the program has the capacity to sustain high quality over time. While having insurance or a sound budget (another policy that does not appear to correlate to high quality) might not be indicative of quality, could an endorsement system give a program its highest rating if they didn't have the policy in place? In other words, if the classroom practices are magnificent but any child who is injured on the playground is stuck with all the medical bills, or the environment is enriched but the program may have to close its doors next month because they don't balance their budget, is the program really functioning at the highest quality?

If you find yourself in the situation where you need to create and adopt a new policy to meet high quality standards it should be looked at in the same way as a classroom improvement: an opportunity to increase the quality of care for children and families. But developing and incorporating a policy is not as simple as typing it up and distributing it, not if you really intend to integrate the policy and practice into your program.

How to Develop a Policy

When developing a new policy, here are a few guidelines to follow:

- For consistency and to ensure all readers know it's a policy, develop a template.
- Answer *what* and *why* as you write the policy.
- Make sure the policy is reflective of the program's overall mission and goals and does not contradict other policies.
- Keep the language clear, concise, and complete to ensure that the reader can fully understand the purpose of the policy.

Policy Example

Sunshine Child Development Center minimizes the spread of infectious diseases and prioritizes the health and safety of the children and staff members while at the program.

How to Write Procedures

When writing procedures, follow these guidelines:

- Develop a template to differentiate procedures from policies (they can also be a part of or attached to the relevant policy).
- Answer *when* and *how* in the procedure.
- Make sure it does not contradict other procedures or the program's mission and goals.

Procedure Example

Sunshine Child development Center will

- *require the use of gloves during all contact with bodily fluids*
- *train staff on universal precautions upon hire and annually thereafter*
- *require everyone to wash their hands upon entering the building*
- *require full compliance with hand washing and diapering procedures*

Note: The policy and procedure examples noted above were not written to meet standards and are not intended to be copied.

Implementing a Policy

Creating policies and procedures is one thing. Implementing them is another. Many programs have written a policy to meet a standard but failed to plan for its implementation. A good example of this is semiannual conferences between families and teachers. This policy is often in writing, but its implementation has not been considered or committed to and therefore doesn't always happen. If you write a policy, you also must plan how it will be implemented and make sure this is explicit in the procedures. Even if an accompanying procedure is not required, it is a good idea to develop one. Ensuring everyone knows how the policy is implemented will help contribute to its implementation.

A Plan for Introducing Policies

Developing a plan for introducing policies may sound unnecessary, but it is a good idea. Will you introduce them at staff meetings? Will you write them into handbooks each year? Will you announce them on a family bulletin board or newsletter? Determine how you will share new or updated policies so they are given the attention and commitment they deserve.

Walk the Walk

As the leader and manager of the program you must set a good example, walk the walk, and talk the talk. When a policy and procedure is in place, you should not only enforce it, you should be its role model. Do you wash your hands every time you enter a room? Do you arrange for fire and disaster drills monthly? Do you offer relevant staff training? Do you follow ratios? If you adhere to policies, new and old, they are more likely to be adopted quickly and effortlessly.

Physical Environment Quick Check

Indicator	Observational Notes	Follow-Up Needed
Materials		
Classroom shelves are well stocked with ample materials.		
The materials are varied, addressing different skill development opportunities.		
Materials are in good repair.		
Materials are accessible to children (not in covered bins or up high).		
There is an ample variety of books in good repair, including nonfiction, fiction, and teacher or child made.		
Materials are available to address all learning domains and appropriate age-level skill development.		
Materials are available to ensure variety in outdoor play.		

Physical Environment Quick Check (cont.)

Indicator	Observational Notes	Follow-Up Needed
Design		
The classroom is divided into distinct learning areas that allow for different sized groups of children to engage.		
Materials are labeled and organized in a way that helps children find them and put them away.		
The decor is child-focused. Children's work and art and real-life photos dominate.		
There are soft and cozy spaces for children to play and relax.		
The room arrangement considers the noise level of different learning centers.		
Upon entering the room, the observer can identify what children are working on and accomplishing in the room based on activity and decor.		

Health and Safety Checklist

- [ ] _____
- [ ] _____
- [ ] _____
- [ ] _____
- [ ] _____
- [ ] _____
- [ ] _____
- [ ] _____
- [ ] _____
- [ ] _____
- [ ] _____
- [ ] _____
- [ ] _____
- [ ] _____
- [ ] _____
- [ ] _____
- [ ] _____
- [ ] _____
- [ ] _____
- [ ] _____

Criteria Evaluation Form

Criteria Number:	Category:
Intent of criteria: (information from self-study materials and staff discussion)	
How we meet the criteria: (practical application of criteria intent)	
Observable evidence (if applicable):	
Documented evidence (if applicable):	
Action plan to meet (if applicable):	

Criteria Number:	Category:
Intent of criteria: (information from self-study materials and staff discussion)	
How we meet the criteria: (practical application of criteria intent)	
Observable evidence (if applicable):	
Documented evidence (if applicable):	
Action plan to meet (if applicable):	

Interactions Self-Quiz

Interactions are one of your most important and effective teaching tools. There is a lot to learn about interactions and how to use them effectively in the classroom. This quiz will help you to see where you are and where you need to go.

Statement	Yes, or most of the time	No, or rarely
I sit and talk with children at meal and snacktimes.		
I allow children to make choices.		
I read to children at least two times every day.		
I sing to children.		
I speak to children at their eye level.		
I ask children questions to find out what they are thinking.		
I ask children questions to find out what they are learning.		
I ask children questions to find out about them.		
I verbally welcome all children, parents, and visitors to my classroom.		
I have conversations with children during routine care, such as during hand washing and diapering.		
I choose my words carefully.		
I use positional words (under, before, next to).		
I use children's names more than nicknames.		
I use words to comfort and reassure.		
I use words to help children describe their thoughts, actions, and feelings, and validate them.		
I use interactions to build children's self-confidence.		
My words are positive and not biased.		
I use open-ended questions and comments.		
When I tell children to use their words, I know they know the words they need.		
I limit my use of the word *no*.		
I explain why even to nonverbal children.		
I use words to solve problems.		
I offer specific praise, such as "I like the choice you made," more often than generic praise, such as "Good job."		

Family Questionnaire

Family primary last name:	Date:
Other family last names:	

We like to stay in touch with our families (for nonemergency reasons) throughout the week. What is your preferred method of communication? (please circle and provide information)

E-mail: _____   Work phone: _____

Cell phone: _____   Other: _____

Child's Development	Objectives for Education Program
Children change, grow, and develop every day. Please share information on your child's current development, likes or dislikes, or discoveries or interests at home.	Every family has different objectives or hopes for their child's experience in an early education program. Tell us about yours.

Family Questionnaire (cont.)

Family Traditions	Program Participation Opportunities
We enjoy learning about different family or holiday traditions. What family or holiday traditions do you have that we could learn more about at school? (For example, a cooking project, song, story, game, or craft.) We also invite family members to visit our center and share these traditions if possible. We welcome parents and guardians, grandparents, aunts and uncles, and other interested people. Please let us know of anyone who may be interested in sharing with our center. Describe traditions here:	We love it when family members join our program. We also understand busy schedules. Please circle any opportunities you would like more information about. • Reading to the class • Preparing materials for activities at home • Donating recyclable items • Planning center events • Helping during classroom special event • Chaperoning field trips • Cooking or craft project support • Collecting dramatic play items • Making bibs or blankets • Sharing information about your work (for example, firefighter, stylist, architect, veterinarian, nurse) or hobby (for example, rock collecting, scrapbooking, photography) • Other _____

Is there anything else you'd like to share with us about your family?

Family Survey

(Questions can be modified to suit your program's needs/characteristics.)

Tell us how we're doing.
Please provide as much detail as you can so we can provide the best care possible.

Question	Please circle your response. 5 = absolutely 1 = not at all	Comments
I feel my child's growth and development is supported.	5 4 3 2 1	
I have a positive relationship with my child's teachers.	5 4 3 2 1	
The amount and type of communication with teachers and management is satisfactory.	5 4 3 2 1	
I feel my child is safe in this environment.	5 4 3 2 1	
I understand what my child is learning and how he/she is developing in the classroom.	5 4 3 2 1	
The program's family events (for example, conferences, special events) are conveniently scheduled.	5 4 3 2 1	
I am satisfied with my level of involvement in the program.	5 4 3 2 1	
I understand and am not surprised by the program policies and procedures (hours, sick child policy, and so on).	5 4 3 2 1	
Someone from management is available and receptive when I need to speak with them.	5 4 3 2 1	
If you would like follow-up on any of these items please provide your name and preferred method of contact.		

Thank you for your time and commitment to our program!

Family and Community Activity Planning Sheet

Month 1:	Month 2:	Month 3:	Month 4:
Family connection:	Family connection:	Family connection:	Family connection:
Community connection:	Community connection:	Community connection:	Community connection:

Month 5:	Month 6:	Month 7:	Month 8:
Family connection:	Family connection:	Family connection:	Family connection:
Community connection:	Community connection:	Community connection:	Community connection:

Month 9:	Month 10:	Month 11:	Month 12:
Family connection:	Family connection:	Family connection:	Family connection:
Community connection:	Community connection:	Community connection:	Community connection:

Ongoing connections (newsletters, for example):

Appendix D:
What's Next

Preparing Teachers for the On-Site Visit #1

Preparing Teachers for the On-Site Visit #2

Preparing Teachers for the On-Site Visit #3

Daily Walkabout Sheet

Preparing Teachers for the On-Site Visit #1

Project 1: Review the Standards

The on-site visit is coming soon! To make sure you are fully prepared for that day, complete this week-long project to highlight how you meet all the classroom standards and criteria. Good luck and have fun!

Attached you will find a copy of the classroom standards and criteria that the representative of _____ will use to assess your classroom practices.

Throughout the week, as you complete your daily tasks and responsibilities, use the table below to describe the things you are doing to meet the classroom standards and criteria.

Classroom Standards	What I'm Doing to Meet the Standards
Health and safety standards:	
Interactions between myself and the children:	
Delivery of my curriculum:	

Classroom Standards	What I'm Doing to Meet the Standards
Assessment of the children's learning:	
The learning environment:	
My teaching practices:	
Communicating with families:	
Connecting with our community:	

Upon completion at the end of the week, please turn in this project to

_____

Thank you for your dedicated time and effort!

Preparing Teachers for the On-Site Visit #2

Project 2: Talk About the Standards

The on-site visit is coming soon! To make sure you are fully prepared for that day, complete this week-long project to highlight how you meet all the classroom standards and criteria. Good luck and have fun!

Attached you will find a copy of the classroom standards and criteria that the representative of _____ will use to assess your classroom practices.

This week you are going to work with another teacher in a different class-room. Together you will create a list of ten questions* about the standards and criteria that you think the representative of _____ might ask during the on-site visit. When you are finished, approach another pair of teachers and conduct your interview using the questions you created. In turn, ask those teachers to interview you and your partner using the questions they created.

1. _____

_____

Answer: _____

_____

_____

_____

2. _____

_____

Answer: _____

_____

_____

_____

3. _____

_____

Answer: _____

_____

_____

_____

4. _____

_____

Answer: _____

_____

_____

_____

5. _____

_____

Answer: _____

_____

_____

_____

6. _____

_____

Answer: _____

_____

_____

_____

7. _____

_____

Answer: _____

_____

_____

_____

8. _____

_____

Answer: _____

_____

_____

_____

9. _____

_____

Answer: _____

_____

_____

_____

10. _____

_____

Answer: _____

_____

_____

_____

Upon completion at the end of the week, please turn in this project to

_____

Thank you for you dedicated time and effort!

---

*An interview with a representative from the third-party quality endorsement system can make anyone feel anxious. However, it doesn't need to cause alarm. All the representative is trying to do is understand something he or she didn't observe, or the representative may want to obtain a more complete picture of something that was observed. This is the interviewee's time to show off and share the amazing things that happen in the classroom or program. Below are a few example questions to get teachers thinking about possible topics a validator may ask about.

Sample Questions for Practice (these are just examples of typical questions, not actual endorsed questions)

- Tell me about how you approach child guidance.
- What kinds of activities do children do on rainy days?
- How do you plan for each day?
- Tell me about how you observe and assess children.
- How are children's special needs supported in your classroom?
- Share with me your typical routine.
- How do you get the families involved in the classroom?
- Tell me about your emergency procedures.
- What do you use your observation notes for?
- What is your program's educational philosophy?
- How do you incorporate those unexpected opportunities for learning into your daily routine?
- How do you encourage the children's reading and writing skills appropriate to this age?
- What role does media play in your program?
- Tell me how you ensure diversity is represented in your classroom.

Preparing Teachers for the On-Site Visit #3

Project Three: The Learning Environment

The on-site visit is coming soon! To make sure you are fully prepared for that day, complete this week-long project to highlight how your classroom environment meets the appropriate standards and criteria. Good luck and have fun!

Attached you will find a copy of the classroom standards and criteria that the representative of _____ will use to assess your classroom practices. Review the standards and criteria and list those that specifically deal with the learning environment of your classroom. Tour your classroom and describe how you have set up your learning environment to meet those standards and criteria.

Learning Environment Standards	What I Have Done to Meet the Standards

Upon completion at the end of the week, please turn in this project to

_____

Thank you for your dedicated time and effort!

Daily Walkabout Sheet

Date: _____

- [ ] The center is clean and inviting.

- [ ] Correct hand-washing procedures are being followed.

- [ ] Correct diapering procedures are being followed.

- [ ] Evidence of communication with families is apparent in each classroom.

- [ ] Evidence of learning is apparent in each classroom.

- [ ] The classroom environments are set up to encourage learning.

- [ ] Sufficient materials are available in each classroom to allow for play and learning.

- [ ] Teachers are encouraging the development of age-appropriate math skills.

- [ ] Teachers are encouraging the development of age-appropriate reading skills.

- [ ] Teachers are encouraging the development of age-appropriate writing skills.

- [ ] Teachers are encouraging the development of problem-solving skills.

- [ ] Age-appropriate child guidance skills are used and are evident.

- [ ] Teachers and children are having meaningful conversations.

- [ ] Teachers are asking age-appropriate open-ended questions.

- [ ] A fair balance of teacher-driven and child-initiated activities are planned for the day.

- [ ] Each classroom has planned for large-motor activities for the day.

- [ ] Evidence of teachers observing children's learning is apparent.

- [ ] Teachers have planned for family involvement in their classroom.

☐ Evidence of respectful representation of diversity within the classroom and the community is apparent.

☐ Each classroom is inviting and child-centered.

Areas of opportunity:

_____

_____

_____

_____

_____

_____

Plan of action for remediation:

_____

_____

_____

_____

_____

_____

References

American Montessori Society. 2008. *School accreditation standards and criteria: School improvement through American Montessori Society school accreditation.* New York: American Montessori Society.

Beich, E., and E. West. 2004. *ASTD training certification manual.* Alexandria, VA: ASTD Publications.

Bentham, Renee. 2008. Rich environments for adult learners. *Young Children* 63 (3): 72–74.

Bergen, Sharon. 2009. *Best practices for training early childhood professionals.* St. Paul, MN: Redleaf Press.

Center for the Child Care Workforce. 2002. Estimating the size and components of the U.S. childcare workforce and caregiving population: Key findings from the Child Care Workforce Estimate. http://www.ccw .org/pubs/workforceestimatereport.pdf.

Commission on International and Trans-Regional Accreditation. 2008. *Standards and quality indicators: Schools, centers, and education providers.* Tempe, AZ: Commission on International and Trans-Regional Accreditation.

Committee on Early Childhood, Adoption, and Dependent Care. 2005. Quality early education and child care from birth to kindergarten. *Pediatrics* 115 (1): 187–91.

Copple, Carol, and Sue Bredekamp, eds. 2009. *Developmentally appropriate practice in early childhood programs serving children from birth through age 8.* 3rd ed. Washington, DC: National Association for the Education of Young Children.

Council of Chief State School Officers. n.d. Assessing child learning and developmental outcomes. Fact sheet. www.ccsso.org/ECEAassessment.

Curtis, Deb, and Margie Carter. 2003. *Designs for living and learning: Transforming early childhood environments.* St. Paul, MN: Redleaf Press.

Galinsky, Ellen, Carollee Howes, Susan Kontos, and Marybeth Shinn. 1994. *The study of children in family child care and relative care: Highlights of findings.* New York: Family and Work Institute.

Harms, Thelma, Richard M. Clifford, and Debby Cryer. 2005. *Early childhood environment rating scale.* Rev. ed. New York: Teachers College Press.

Helburn, Suzanne W., ed. 1995. Cost, quality, and child outcomes in child care centers. Public report. Denver: Economics Department, University of Colorado.

Herzenberg, Stephan, Mark Price, and David Bradley. 2005. Losing ground in early childhood education: Declining workforce qualifications in an expanding industry. Executive summary. Washington, DC: Economic Policy Institute. http://epi.3cdn.net/9d5bb2f76defdffcac_vxm6bk05i.pdf.

Hyson, Marilou. 2008. *Enthusiastic and engaged learners: Approaches to learning in the early childhood classroom.* New York: Teachers College Press.

Katz, Lilian. 1993. Multiple perspectives on the quality of early childhood programs. *Eric Digest* ED355041. Urbana, IL: ERIC Clearinghouse on Elementary and Early Childhood Education.

Kelley, Pamela, and Gregory Camilli. 2007. The impact of teacher education on outcomes in center-based early childhood programs: A meta-analysis. Working paper. http://nieer.org/resources/research/TeacherEd.pdf.

Lee, Kathy. 2003. *Solutions for early childhood directors: Real answers to everyday challenges.* Beltsville, MD: Gryphon House.

National Accreditation Commission. 2007. *Accreditation for the 21st century: Trainer's guide.* Austin, TX: National Association of Child Care Professionals.

National Association for the Education of Young Children. n.d. NAEYC accreditation: The right choice for kids. http://www.rightchoice forkids.org.

National Association for the Education of Young Children. 2005a. *Curriculum: A guide to the NAEYC early childhood program standard and related accreditation criteria.* Washington, DC: National Association for the Education of Young Children.

———.2005b. *Health: A guide to the NAEYC early childhood program standards and related accreditation criteria.* Washington, DC: National Association for the Education of Young Children.

———. 2005c. *NAEYC early childhood program standards and accreditation criteria: The mark of quality in early childhood education.* Washington, DC: National Association for the Education of Young Children.

———. 2005d. *Physical environment: A guide to the NAEYC early childhood program standard and related accreditation criteria.* Washington, DC: National Association for the Education of Young Children.

———. 2005e. *Relationships: A guide to the NAEYC early childhood program standard and related accreditation criteria.* Washington, DC: National Association for the Education of Young Children.

———. 2005f. *Teaching: A guide to the NAEYC early childhood program standard and related accreditation criteria.* Washington, DC: National Association for the Education of Young Children.

National Association for the Education of Young Children and the National Association of Early Childhood Specialists in State Departments of Education. 2003. Early childhood curriculum, assessment, and program administration: Building an effective, accountable system in programs for children birth through age 8. Joint position statement. http://naecs.crc .uiuc.edu/position/pscape.html.

National Association for Regulatory Administration and the National Child Care Information and Technical Assistance Center. 2005. The 2005 child care licensing study. http://nara.affiniscape.com/associations/4734/ files/2005%20Licensing%20Study%20Final%20Report_Web.pdf.

National Center for the Early Childhood Work Force. 1997. NAEYC accreditation as a strategy for improving child care quality: An assessment by the National Center for the Early Childhood Work Force. Primary investigators Marcy Whitebrook, Laura Sakai, and Carollee Howes. http://www.ccw.org/pubs/naeyc.pdf.

National Child Care Staffing Study. 1989. Who cares? Child care teachers and the quality of care in America. Primary investigators Marcy Whitebrook, Carollee Howes, and Deborah Phillips. Oakland, CA: Child Care Employee Project.

National Early Childhood Program Accreditation. 2005. What it means to you. http://www.necpa.net/whatitmeanstoyou.html.

National Early Childhood Program Accreditation Commission. 1994. *NECPA self assessment instrument.* Mount Pleasant, SC: National Early Childhood Program Accreditation.

Peisner-Feinber, E. S., M. R. Burchinal, R. M. Clifford, M. L. Culkin, C. Howes, S. L. Kagan, N. Yazejian, P. Byler, J, Rustici, and J. Zelazo. 1999. The children of the cost, quality, and outcomes study go to school. Executive summary. http://www.fpg.unc.edu/~ncedl/PDFs/CQO-es.pdf.

Pianta, R. C. 1999. *Enhancing relationships between children and teachers.* Washington, DC: American Psychological Association.

University of Maryland. 2008. Effective communication. http://www.health.umd.edu/fsap/communication.html.

World Health Organization. 1948. Preamble to the constitution of the World Health Organization. In *Official records of the World Health Organization,* vol. 2, 100. Geneva, Switzerland. Quoted in National Association for the Education of Young Children. 2005c.

Notes

Notes